Current
CONTROVERSIES

Animal Rights

Other Books in the Current Controversies Series

Animal Rights

Noah Berlatsky, Book Editor

GREENHAVEN PRESS

A part of Gale, Cengage Learning

Farmington Hills, Mich • San Francisco • New York • Waterville, Maine
Meriden, Conn • Mason, Ohio • Chicago

Patricia Coryell, *Vice President & Publisher, New Products & GVRL*
Douglas Dentino, *Manager, New Products*
Judy Galens, *Acquisitions Editor*

For more information, contact:
Greenhaven Press
27500 Drake Rd.
Farmington Hills, MI 48331-3535
Or you can visit our Internet site at gale.cengage.com

For product information and technology assistance, contact us at

Gale Customer Support, 1-800-877-4253
For permission to use material from this text or product, submit all requests online at www.cengage.com/permissions

Further permissions questions can be emailed to permissionrequest@cengage.com

Articles in Greenhaven Press anthologies are often edited for length to meet page requirements. In addition, original titles of these works are changed to clearly present the main thesis and to explicitly indicate the author's opinion. Every effort is made to ensure that Greenhaven Press accurately reflects the original intent of the authors. Every effort has been made to trace the owners of copyrighted material.

Cover image © She/Shutterstock.com.

LIBRARY OF CONGRESS CATALOGING-IN-PUBLICATION DATA

Animal rights / Noah Berlatsky, book editor.
    pages cm. -- (Current controversies)
    Includes bibliographical references and index.
    ISBN 978-0-7377-7207-4 (hardcover) -- ISBN 978-0-7377-7208-1 (pbk.)
    1. Animal rights. 2. Human-animal relationships. 3. Animal welfare. I. Berlatsky, Noah.
    HV4708.A5427 2015
    179'.3--dc23
                                               2014041213

Printed in the United States of America
1 2 3 4 5   19 18 17 16 15

Contents

Chapter 1: Does Scientific Testing Violate Animal Rights?

Yes: Scientific Testing Violates Animal Rights

There has been an increase in the United States in the use of nonhuman primates in testing in recent years, both because there is a surplus of such primates and because it is thought that primates are a better subject for research testing than other animals, like rodents. However, primates can experience severe distress from testing, and there is little evidence that they provide corresponding benefits. Just as the use of chimpanzees has been greatly reduced because of ethical concerns and the development of testing alternatives, so should scientists reduce testing on other nonhuman primates.

No: Scientific Testing Does Not Violate Animal Rights

Animal testing is necessary for medical advancement in areas like cancer and pain treatment. Moreover, it is hypocritical to protest at the scientific testing of animals when chickens and farm animals live in worse conditions and are slaughtered in far greater numbers. However, scientific testing does raise ethical issues, and it is important for scientists to continue to honestly justify the pain and suffering they cause animals to the public, so that such pain and suffering does not become routine or ignorable.

Research on nonhuman primates is very controversial and very costly. As a result, some scientists and some schools have abandoned nonhuman primate research altogether. However, nonhuman primate research is very important in diverse areas, including addiction, behavioral research, spinal research, and reproductive research—all areas in which primates' close connection to human behavior and biology is invaluable. Researchers who use primates therefore work to minimize cost and harm to the animals even as they continue with necessary research.

Chapter 2: Does Factory Farming Violate Animal Rights?

Academic critics often argue that so-called industrial farming is inefficient, cruel, and damaging to the environment. These critics have little sense of the day-to-day reality of farming, or of the important hands-on experience farmers bring to their work. Factory farming practices are often more humane, efficient, and environmentally sound than supposedly organic alternatives. Factory farming is necessary to feed the world's population, and critics should pay attention to farmers' expertise rather than push for changes that may have unexpected negative consequences.

Chapter 3: Does Hunting Violate Animal Rights?

Hunting causes pain and suffering to animals, which are often wounded rather than killed outright. In many cases, hunting leaves young animals to starve to death on their own or separates mates and offspring. Hunting does not promote conservation but instead causes a distortion of ecosystems as certain species are encouraged and predator species are killed or discouraged. As such, hunting is inhumane and unnecessary and should be eliminated.

The killing of baby seals in Canada is cruel, bloody, and ugly. Most Canadians oppose the practice, yet the Canadian government subsidizes and supports it through tax breaks and technical help. This is because the seal industry is well-positioned politically. However, as more countries close their markets to seal pelts and global warming reduces the seal harvest, it is a good moment to reconsider seal hunting. The government could provide a one-time buyout of the seal industry and end the practice of seal hunting as it ended whale hunting.

No: Hunting Does Not Violate Animal Rights

In modern times, people are disconnected from the production of food. This makes it difficult to think usefully about sustainable practices and about human connection to the natural world. Hunting connects people to premodern ways of understanding food slaughter and production. It is also very sustainable, even compared to organic farming, in which many animals are killed inadvertently and habitat is destroyed. Hunting therefore offers one of the few ways for modern people to reconnect with wildlife and earlier modes of food production.

The Faroe Islands whale kill is an extremely old tradition, going back more than one thousand years. It results in the death of a very small percentage of pilot whales and is an important part of Faroe Islands culture. Environmental activists would do better to focus their attention on large-scale industrial killing of fish and pollution of the oceans. These are more serious threats to larger numbers of aquatic creatures and the health of our planet.

Britain's so-called Hunting Act of 2004, which bans many kinds of hunting with dogs in England and Wales, was supposed to improve animal welfare. However, hunting with dogs can help manage fox and other predators and results in healthier populations of wildlife. There have been few studies of the health of the animal population following the passage of the Hunting Act, and what evidence is available suggests that banning hunting has hurt wildlife. The opposition to hunting is based on prejudice, rather than on science or facts.

Chapter 4: Does Using Animals for Entertainment Violate Their Rights?

No: Using Animals for Entertainment Does Not Violate Their Rights

Foreword

By definition, controversies are "discussions of questions in which opposing opinions clash" (*Webster's Twentieth Century Dictionary Unabridged*). Few would deny that controversies are a pervasive part of the human condition and exist on virtually every level of human enterprise. Controversies transpire between individuals and among groups, within nations and between nations. Controversies supply the grist necessary for progress by providing challenges and challengers to the status quo. They also create atmospheres where strife and warfare can flourish. A world without controversies would be a peaceful world; but it also would be, by and large, static and prosaic.

The Series' Purpose

The purpose of the Current Controversies series is to explore many of the social, political, and economic controversies dominating the national and international scenes today. Titles selected for inclusion in the series are highly focused and specific. For example, from the larger category of criminal justice, Current Controversies deals with specific topics such as police brutality, gun control, white collar crime, and others. The debates in Current Controversies also are presented in a useful, timeless fashion. Articles and book excerpts included in each title are selected if they contribute valuable, long-range ideas to the overall debate. And wherever possible, current information is enhanced with historical documents and other relevant materials. Thus, while individual titles are current in focus, every effort is made to ensure that they will not become quickly outdated. Books in the Current Controversies series will remain important resources for librarians, teachers, and students for many years.

In addition to keeping the titles focused and specific, great care is taken in the editorial format of each book in the series. Book introductions and chapter prefaces are offered to provide background material for readers. Chapters are organized around several key questions that are answered with diverse opinions representing all points on the political spectrum. Materials in each chapter include opinions in which authors clearly disagree as well as alternative opinions in which authors may agree on a broader issue but disagree on the possible solutions. In this way, the content of each volume in Current Controversies mirrors the mosaic of opinions encountered in society. Readers will quickly realize that there are many viable answers to these complex issues. By questioning each author's conclusions, students and casual readers can begin to develop the critical thinking skills so important to evaluating opinionated material.

Current Controversies is also ideal for controlled research. Each anthology in the series is composed of primary sources taken from a wide gamut of informational categories including periodicals, newspapers, books, US and foreign government documents, and the publications of private and public organizations. Readers will find factual support for reports, debates, and research papers covering all areas of important issues. In addition, an annotated table of contents, an index, a book and periodical bibliography, and a list of organizations to contact are included in each book to expedite further research.

Perhaps more than ever before in history, people are confronted with diverse and contradictory information. During the Persian Gulf War, for example, the public was not only treated to minute-to-minute coverage of the war, it was also inundated with critiques of the coverage and countless analyses of the factors motivating US involvement. Being able to sort through the plethora of opinions accompanying today's major issues, and to draw one's own conclusions, can be a complicated and frustrating struggle. It is the editors' hope that Current Controversies will help readers with this struggle.

Introduction

> *"The main driver of species extinction is destruction of habitat as human dwellings, agriculture, and industry spread across the world, cannibalizing areas where animals used to thrive."*

The issue of animal rights usually focuses on the welfare and treatment of animals as individuals. However, humans also can have broad, wide-scale impacts on animals as species. In fact, ecologists are concerned that humans are changing the planet in ways that are making it uninhabitable for many other creatures.

According to Christine Dell'Amore, writing in *National Geographic*, the current rate of species extinction is a thousand times higher on earth than it would be without human interference.[1] Dell'Amore cites a study by Stuart Pimm, a conservation ecologist at Duke University. Pimm calculated that about one hundred to one thousand species are lost per million species each year. Most of these extinctions are because of human-caused habitat destruction and global warming or climate change. Before humans evolved, Pimm argues, less than one species per million became extinct every year. Pimm believes the extinction rate will continue to climb, leading to a mass extinction event on earth, the sixth in our planet's history.

The last extinction event occurred around sixty-six million years ago, according to former vice president Al Gore, in a re-

---

1. Christine Dell'Amore, "Species Extinction Happening 1,000 Times Faster Because of Humans?," *National Geographic*, May 29, 2014. http://news.nationalgeographic.com /news/2014/05/140529-conservation-science-animals-species-endangered-extinction.

view of Elizabeth Kolbert's book *The Sixth Extinction*.[2] At that time, a six-mile-wide asteroid hit the earth, killing the dinosaurs and eliminating fully three-quarters of all plant and animal species. "This time," Gore says, "a giant asteroid isn't to blame—we are, by altering environmental conditions on our planet so swiftly and dramatically that a large proportion of other species cannot adapt. And we are risking our own future as well, by fundamentally altering the integrity of the climate balance that has persisted in more or less the same configuration since the end of the last ice age, and which has fostered the flourishing of human civilization."[3]

As Gore suggests, the main driver of species extinction is destruction of habitat as human dwellings, agriculture, and industry spread across the world, cannibalizing areas where animals used to thrive. Another threat is climate change, which many experts believe is being driven by human-induced carbon dioxide emissions, which enter the atmosphere and raise the temperature of the earth. Zoë Schlanger at *Newsweek* writes that "the concentration of carbon dioxide in the atmosphere is the highest it has been in at least 800,000 years, and the ocean, which absorbs vast amounts of that gas, is acidifying at an alarming rate."[4] The fear is that ocean food chains will be unable to withstand the acidification, and marine species will be wiped out altogether.

Among the most dramatic species extinction events is the dying off of bees worldwide. In the last five years, 30 percent of American bees have died, and a third of all bee colonies in the United States have been destroyed. The exact cause of the

2. Al Gore, "Without a Trace," *New York Times*, February 10, 2014. http://www.nytimes.com/2014/02/16/books/review/the-sixth-extinction-by-elizabeth-kolbert.html.

3. Ibid.

4. Zoë Schlanger, "Earth Heading for Another Mass Extinction, Scientists Warn," *Newsweek*, May 30, 2014. http://www.newsweek.com/earth-heading-another-mass-extinction-scientists-warn-252835.

massive bee die-off is unclear. Joachim Hagopian at the Centre for Research on Globalization notes that "a new government study blames a combination of factors for the mysterious and dramatic loss of honeybees, including increased use of pesticides especially in the US, shrinking habitats, multiple viruses, poor nutrition and genetics, and even cell phone towers."[5] Hagopian suggests that the combination of the Varroa destructor, an insecticide-resistant mite, and bee immune systems weakened by insecticides may be the culprit. In any case, the bee die-off has serious consequences for humans as well as for the bees themselves. The insects are vital to human agriculture, since 80 percent of US food crops are pollinated by bees.

Another group of animals that are facing catastrophic losses is amphibians. A 2013 study by Michael Adams of the US Geological Survey found that frogs and related amphibians are seeing their numbers drop by 3.7 percent a year. That means that they could vanish from half of the habitats they currently occupy in the United States in twenty-six years. Certain especially threatened species are disappearing even faster.

As with bees, the exact cause of the amphibian die-off is not clear and may be linked to multiple factors. These include pollution, loss of habitat, climate change, and a particularly deadly fungal infection. John R. Platt, writing in *Scientific American*, said that researchers have found that even amphibians in protected areas seem to be affected, which is disturbing. Platt quotes Michael Adams as saying, "The fact that amphibian declines are occurring in our most protected areas adds weight to the hypothesis that this is a global phenomenon with implications for managers of all kinds of land-

---

5. Joachim Hagopian, "Death and Extinction of Bees," *Global Research*, March 28, 2014. http://www.globalresearch.ca/death-and-extinction-of-the-bees/5375684.

scapes, even protected ones."[6] The inability to isolate causes and the widespread nature of the problem increase fears that amphibians, like bees and marine life, may be slipping toward a species die-off that is irreversible.

The remainder of this book looks at other issues of animal rights and welfare in such chapters as "Does Scientific Testing Violate Animal Rights?," "Does Factory Farming Violate Animal Rights?," "Does Hunting Violate Animal Rights?," and "Does Using Animals for Entertainment Violate Their Rights?" Each section examines the ethics of human/animal interactions and probes how people can, or should, live with other creatures on this planet.

7. Quoted in John R. Platt, "Amphibians in U.S. Declining at 'Alarming and Rapid Rate,'" *Scientific American*, May 23, 2013. http://blogs.scientificamerican.com /extinction-countdown/2013/05/23/amphibians-declining-alarming.

CHAPTER 1

Does Scientific Testing Violate Animal Rights?

Chapter Preface

Students in high school science classes traditionally dissect animals. According to the website Anima*learn*, the total number of vertebrates dissected every year in high schools is probably around six million. Frogs are the animals that are most dissected, but dissection of fetal pigs and cats is also common. Other animals that may be dissected include dogfish sharks, perch, pigeons, salamanders, and rabbits.

Many animal rights proponents and groups argue that the mass killing of animals for dissection is inhumane, cruel, and unnecessary. People for the Ethical Treatment of Animals (PETA), for example, argues that animals used for dissection are sometimes killed in inhumane ways—they may be injected with formaldehyde as a preservative before they are actually dead, resulting in severe pain. PETA also maintains that "classroom dissection desensitizes students to the sanctity of life."[1] Students are often initially reluctant to perform dissections; requiring and encouraging them to do so can lead to a greater "callousness" toward the suffering of animals.

Animal rights groups also argue that dissection is unnecessary. Today computer programs can simulate dissection, allowing students to learn about anatomy without having to dissect actual animals. In some cases, animal welfare groups have offered to provide software to high schools that agree to give up dissection. This may be a benefit from a purely financial perspective; ABC News reporter Ned Potter notes that "dissecting frogs—whether or not teachers value the experience their students get from seeing an animal's organs—is a costly proposi-

---

1. PETA, "Dissection: Lessons in Cruelty," accessed July 18, 2014. http://www.peta.org /issues/animals-used-for-experimentation/animals-used- experimentation-factsheets /dissection-lessons-cruelty.

tion for many schools," given the expense of purchasing animals and maintaining a lab.[2]

Despite the high cost and the animal rights concerns, there are some proponents of high school dissections. Kaitlyn Boettcher, writing for the website Mental Floss, notes that many teachers believe "that if students see and feel these organ systems for themselves, they will take more out of the lesson than if the teacher just lectured or assigned readings about it."[3] The National Science Teachers Association (NSTA) "supports each teacher's decision to use animal dissection activities" to allow students to learn about specific organisms and improve their observational skills.[4] NSTA says that ethical treatment of animals is imperative and should be balanced with the potential for learning.

The rest of this chapter looks at other controversies around animals and science, especially the use of animals and primates in scientific research and drug testing.

2. Ned Potter, "Save the Frogs: Animal Rights Groups Help High Schools Do Frog Dissections by Computer Program," ABC News, June 1, 2011. http://abcnews.go.com /Technology/save-frogs-animal-rights-groups-offer-schools-free/story?id=13728046.

3. Kaitlyn Boettcher, "Why Do Students Dissect Frogs?," Mental Floss, May 9, 2013. http://mentalfloss.com/article/49855/why-do-students-dissect-frogs.

4. NSTA, "NSTA Position Statement: Responsible Use of Live Animals and Dissection in the Science Classroom," March 2008. http://www.nsta.org/about/positions /animals.aspx.

Animal Testing Is Cruel

Hope Ferdowsian

Hope Ferdowsian is a physician and director of research policy at the Physicians Committee for Responsible Medicine.

When you burn your finger, the grimace on your face sends a universal message. From Finland to Fiji, virtually any human on earth need only see your face to know that you're in pain. Facial expressions, anthropologists have long known, are an international language.

Torturing Mice

But that language, it turns out, isn't exclusive to humans. Mice also express pain through facial expressions—and those grimaces are remarkably similar to yours or mine, according to a recent article published in the journal *Nature Methods*.

In that extremely controversial study, researchers used a wide range of methods to subject mice to various levels of pain. They immersed the animals' tails in hot water, used radiant heat on them, attached a binder clip to their tails, injected irritants into their feet, induced bladder inflammation with a chemical that causes painful cystitis in humans, and injected acetic acid, causing the mice to develop abdominal constriction and writhe. They performed surgery on the mice and did not provide postoperative analgesics.

The study's authors developed a Mouse Grimace Scale as a measurement tool to help quantify the level of pain experienced by mice. They concluded that when subjected to painful stimuli, mice showed discomfort through facial expressions in the same way humans do.

This painful experiment raised many questions among researchers. Criticism of the study was covered in a newsletter called *Laboratory Animal Welfare Compliance* and elsewhere. Critics have maintained that the experiments were cruel and unnecessary.

The Animal Welfare Act

That study—and the debate surrounding it—highlights critical issues relevant to animal research. For example, mice are now the most commonly used animals in research, but they are not covered by the Animal Welfare Act, one of the few legal protections afforded by U.S. law to other animals used in laboratory experiments.

The original intent of the Laboratory Animal Welfare Act of 1966 was to prevent the unauthorized buying and selling of pet dogs or cats for research purposes. However, the types of enterprises covered, species of animals regulated, reporting requirements, and minimal animal-care guidelines were expanded in subsequent amendments.

Although those laws provide basic protections for some animals used in research, there are significant inconsistencies among U.S. regulations. For example, more than 90 percent of animals used in research are excluded from the Animal Welfare Act.

> *Animals have their own set of needs, and . . . those needs are compromised when humans use animals in laboratory experiments.*

The law excludes birds, rats of the genus *Rattus*, mice of the genus *Mus*, and farm animals. Those exclusions are thought to be primarily attributable to the laboratory industry's successful lobbying efforts. In addition, there is no legal threshold for how much pain and suffering an animal can be exposed to in experiments.

Those were some of the issues discussed at a recent conference on animal research and alternatives. My colleagues at the Physicians Committee for Responsible Medicine and I organized "Animals, Research, and Alternatives" to bring together experts with diverse opinions to discuss animal-research issues. As a physician concerned about the prevention and alleviation of suffering in both humans and animals, I wanted to help facilitate informed, intelligent discussion about animal research.

Despite well over a century of debate, the ethical and scientific-issues surrounding animal research have rarely been studied together in a balanced, organized forum. At our conference, more than 20 speakers shared expertise on the scientific, legal, ethical, and political imperatives regarding animal research.

The first presenter, John Gluck, a professor emeritus of psychology at the University of New Mexico and an affiliate faculty member at Georgetown University's Kennedy Institute of Ethics, set the tone for the conference. After years of conducting primate research, he began studying the ethics of animal research. He and other speakers explained that animals have their own set of needs, and that those needs are compromised when humans use animals in laboratory experiments.

A Politicized Process

Unlike human-research protections, which are now guided by a principled approach, laws governing the use of animals in research have resulted from a largely politicized, patchwork process. That has led to unclear and disparate policies. Meanwhile, studies have dramatically increased our understanding of animal cognition and emotion, suggesting that animals' potential for experiencing harm may be greater than has been appreciated, and that current protections need to be reconsidered.

Although today's laws require institutional committee systems to monitor animal research, individuals serving on Institutional Animal Care and Use Committees have no clear set of ethical principles in which to ground decisions about protocol approval. The scientific question being researched takes precedence over the welfare of the animals. This differs significantly from human-research protections, wherein the interests of individuals and populations are protected, sometimes to the detriment of the scientific question.

At the conference, we learned about intriguing advances in medical research, including a surrogate human immune system for predicting vaccine safety, and a revolutionary approach to breast-cancer research.

Susan Love, president of the Dr. Susan Love Research Foundation, which focuses on eradicating breast cancer, explained that most breast-cancer research in the field is still conducted on animals, even though humans are one of only a few species that develop breast cancer. She discussed the goal of the Army of Women (a partnership between the Avon Foundation for Women and Love's foundation) to challenge research scientists to move from ineffective animal models to breast-cancer-prevention research conducted on healthy women.

Invasive research involving cetaceans can result in confinement and social deprivation, stress and disease, mortality, and destruction of social cultures.

If we could better understand the factors that increase the risk for breast cancer, as well as methods for effective prevention, fewer women would require treatment for breast cancer. But animal experiments do not offer reliable and reproducible findings that can appropriately be applied to women. Whereas animal research is largely investigator-initiated, the Army of Women model tries to address the questions that are central to the care of women at risk for or affected by breast cancer. The model has facilitated the recruitment of women for studies such as a national project backed by the National Institutes of Health and the National Institute of Environmental Health to examine how environment and genes affect breast-cancer risk. This critical study, which began in 2002, could not have been accomplished with animal research.

William Warren explained a surrogate in-vitro human immune system that his company has developed to help predict an individual's immune response to a particular drug or vaccine. The system essentially functions as a clinical trial in a test tube. In other words, it is a virtual human immune system that relies on human immune responses, which differ from those of other animals. The system includes a blood-donor base of hundreds of individuals from diverse populations. It can replace the use of animals for a range of research purposes, most notably vaccine testing. Technologies like those offered by this system could help accelerate the process of developing an HIV vaccine and other immunizations.

Other presenters addressed more of the ethical reasons for moving toward nonanimal alternatives. Lori Marino, a senior lecturer in neuroscience and behavioral biology at Emory University, discussed her noninvasive research on dolphin and whale cognition. She described how invasive research involving cetaceans can result in confinement and social deprivation, stress and disease, mortality, and destruction of social cultures. Although both invasive and noninvasive cetacean research attempts to better understand marine-animal cognition, Marino's research does not involve medical procedures, such as biopsy darting, or techniques that manipulate the mind, social milieu, or physical freedom of the animals.

Animal Lives Matter

Jaak Panksepp, a neuroscientist at Washington State University, discussed the overwhelming evidence that animals experience basic emotions. For example, mice like to be tickled, much as humans do. If our ears were sufficiently attuned, we could hear their laughter. Marc Bekoff, a professor emeritus of ecology and evolutionary biology at the University of Colorado at Boulder, pointed out that the emotional and moral lives of animals matter.

It is now widely acknowledged that animals do suffer, Bekoff explained. Decades of observational and experimental research have provided evidence that animals experience physical pain. Psychological suffering—chronic fear, anxiety, and distress—is another major issue, possibly the most neglected one in animal research.

Researchers have described signs of depression in animals, including nonhuman primates, dogs, pigs, cats, birds, and rodents, among others.

Perhaps Jeremy Bentham (1748–1832), a legal scholar and social reformer, said it best: "The question is not, 'Can they reason?' nor, 'Can they talk?' but rather, 'Can they suffer?'"

Because animals are sentient beings, they share many qualities with humans. For example, animals demonstrate coordinated responses to pain and many emotional states similar to those of humans. Further, the structures and neuroendocrine mechanisms associated with certain psychiatric conditions are shared across a wide range of animals.

Based on these neuroanatomical and physiological similarities, researchers have described signs of depression in animals, including nonhuman primates, dogs, pigs, cats, birds, and rodents, among others. Learned helplessness, a form of depression that has been described in human patient populations such as victims of domestic violence, has also been identified in rodents, dogs, monkeys, and apes exposed to inescapable shocks. Post-traumatic stress disorder and depression have been described in chimpanzees.

The absence of certain neuroanatomical structures may also be significant because animals with less-organized neural circuits may have more-limited coping mechanisms useful in reducing the level of pain they feel. Other animal qualities may also be ethically relevant. For example, many animals demonstrate language skills, complex problem-solving abilities, empathy, and self-awareness.

At the conference, I presented my own observational study of chimpanzees. My colleagues and I have found that many chimpanzees who were used in laboratory research continue to exhibit symptoms of depression and post-traumatic stress disorder years after they have been released to sanctuaries.

Because the United States is the last nation conducting large-scale, invasive experiments on chimpanzees, we have to ask ourselves why—particularly when chimpanzee research has hit a dead end for humans. More than two decades of HIV-vaccine research using chimpanzees has failed to produce a human vaccine. The story is similar for hepatitis C. Hepatitis behaves very differently in humans than in chimpanzees. Chimpanzees are rarely affected by chronic hepatitis or complications associated with hepatitis, such as cirrhosis or hepatocellular carcinoma. Decades of cancer, malaria, cardiovascular disease, and other forms of research using chimpanzees have led to similar failures.

Meanwhile, chimpanzees have demonstrated their own rich preferences in life, including seeking solitude, experiencing new places, living free from fear of attack, and maintaining life-long contact with individuals they love.

The subject of animal research is complex. Each of our own opinions has been informed by education, experience, and personal perspective. Conversations surrounding the use of animals in research are understandably truncated by emotion. Often it seems like two sides talking past each other.

It's clear that we're making progress toward replacing the use of animals in invasive experiments, but we have a lot of work ahead of us. I am hopeful that our conference advanced the dialogue and will contribute to scientific and ethical progress for both people and animals.

In years to come, when we have replaced animals in research, future generations will look back and wonder why this advance did not happen sooner. But they will also be thankful for those who made animals' lives better and strove for better, more ethical science.

Animal Testing Is Bad Science

PETA

PETA (People for the Ethical Treatment of Animals) is an animal rights organization based in the United States.

Animal experimenters want us to believe that if they gave up their archaic habit, sick children and other disease and accident victims would drop dead in droves. But the most significant trend in modern research in recent years has been the recognition that animals rarely serve as good models for the human body.

Wasting Lives

Studies published in prestigious medical journals have shown time and again that animal experimenters are often wasting lives—both animal and human—and precious resources by trying to infect animals with diseases that they would never normally contract. Fortunately, a wealth of cutting-edge, non-animal research methodologies promises a brighter future for both animal and human health. The following are some statements supporting animal experimentation followed by the arguments against them.

"Every major medical advance is attributable to experiments on animals."

This is simply not true. An article published in the esteemed *Journal of the Royal Society of Medicine* has even evaluated this very claim and concluded that it was not supported by any evidence. Most animal experiments are not relevant to human health, they do not contribute meaningfully to medical advances and many are undertaken simply out of curiosity and do not even pretend to hold promise for curing illnesses.

The only reason people are under the misconception that animal experiments help humans is because the media, experimenters, universities and lobbying groups exaggerate the potential of animal experiments to lead to new cures and the role they have played in past medical advances.

People Testing

"If we didn't use animals, we'd have to test new drugs on people."

The fact is that we already *do* test new drugs on people. No matter how many animal tests are undertaken, someone will always be the first human to be tested on. Because animal tests are so unreliable, they make those human trials all the more risky. The Food and Drug Administration (FDA) has noted that 92 percent of all drugs that are shown to be safe and effective in animal tests fail in human trials because they don't work or are dangerous. And of the small percentage that are approved for human use, half are relabeled because of side effects that were not identified in animal tests.

"We have to observe the complex interactions of cells, tissues, and organs in living animals."

While funding for animal experimentation and the number of animals tested on continues to increase, the United States still ranks 49th in the world in life expectancy and second worst in infant mortality in the developed world.

Taking a *healthy* being from a completely different species, artificially inducing a condition that he or she would never normally contract, keeping him or her in an unnatural and distressful environment, and trying to apply the results to naturally occurring diseases in human beings is dubious at best. Physiological reactions to drugs vary enormously from species to species. Penicillin kills guinea pigs but is inactive in rabbits; aspirin kills cats and causes birth defects in rats, mice, guinea pigs, dogs, and monkeys; and morphine, a depressant in humans, stimulates goats, cats, and horses. Further, animals in laboratories typically display behavior indicating extreme psychological distress, and experimenters acknowledge that the use of these stressed-out animals jeopardizes the validity of the data produced.

"Animals help in the fight against cancer."

Since President Richard Nixon signed the Conquest of Cancer Act in 1971, the "war on cancer" in the United States has become a series of losing battles. Through taxes, donations, and private funding, Americans have spent almost $200 billion on cancer research since 1971. However, more than 500,000 Americans die of cancer every year, a 73 percent increase in the death rate since the "war" began.

The Failures of Testing

"Science has a responsibility to use animals to keep looking for cures for all the horrible diseases that people suffer from."

Every year in the United States, animal experimentation gobbles up billions of dollars (including 40 percent of all research funding from the U.S. National Institutes of Health), and more than $1 trillion is spent on health care. While funding for animal experimentation and the number of animals tested on continues to increase, the United States still ranks 49th in the world in life expectancy and second worst in infant mortality in the developed world. While rates of heart disease and strokes have shown slight declines recently—because of lifestyle factors such as diet and smoking rather than any medical advances—cancer rates continue to rise, while alcohol- and drug-treatment centers, prenatal care programs, community mental health clinics, and trauma units continue to suffer closures because they lack sufficient funds.

"Many experiments are not painful to animals and are therefore justified."

The only U.S. law that governs the use of animals in laboratories—the Animal Welfare Act—allows animals to be burned, shocked, poisoned, isolated, starved, forcibly restrained, addicted to drugs, and brain-damaged. No experiment, no matter how painful or trivial, is prohibited—and pain-killers are not even required. Even when alternatives to the use of animals are available, the law does not require that they be used—and often they aren't. Because the Act specifically excludes rats, mice, birds and cold-blooded animals, more than 95 percent of the animals used in laboratories are not subject to the minimal protections provided by federal laws. Because they are not protected by the law, experimenters don't even have to provide mice and rats with pain relief.

Other Options

"We don't want to use animals, but we don't have any other options."

Today, one can even become a board-certified surgeon without harming any animals.

Human clinical and epidemiological studies, human tissue- and cell-based research methods, cadavers, sophisticated high-fidelity human patient simulators and computational models are more reliable, more precise, less expensive, and more humane than animal experiments. Progressive scientists have used human brain cells to develop a model "microbrain," which can be used to study tumors, as well as artificial skin and bone marrow. We can now test irritancy on protein membranes, produce and test vaccines using human tissue, and perform pregnancy tests using blood samples instead of killing rabbits. Animal experiments don't persist because they are the best science, they persist because of experimenters' personal biases and archaic traditions.

"Don't medical students have to dissect animals?"

Nearly 95% of U.S. medical schools—including Yale, Harvard and Stanford—do not use any animals to train medical students and experience with animal dissection or experimentation on live animals is not required or expected of those applying to medical school. Medical students are trained with a combination of didactic methods, sophisticated human patient simulators, interactive computer programs, safe human-based learning methods and clinical experience. Today, one can even become a board-certified surgeon without harming any animals. Some medical professional organizations like the American Board of Anesthesiologists even require physicians to complete simulation training—not animal laboratories—to become board-certified.

"Animals are here for humans to use. If we have to sacrifice 1,000 or 100,000 animals in the hope of benefiting one child, it's worth it."

If experimenting on one intellectually-disabled person could benefit 1,000 children, would we do it? Of course not! Ethics dictate that the value of each life in and of itself cannot be superseded by its potential value to anyone else.

The Case for Phasing Out Experiments on Primates

Kathleen M. Conlee and Andrew N. Rowan

Kathleen M. Conlee is vice president for animal research issues with The Humane Society of the United States (HSUS). Andrew N. Rowan is president and chief executive officer of Humane Society International, and serves as chief international officer and chief scientific officer for HSUS.

Whether they realize it or not, most stakeholders in the debate about using animals for research agree on the common goal of seeking an end to research that causes animals harm.[1] The central issues in the controversy are about *how much* effort should be devoted to that goal and *when* we might reasonably expect to achieve it. Some progress has already been made: The number of animals used for research is about half what it was in the 1970s, and biomedical research has reached the point where we can reasonably begin to envision a time when it could advance without causing harm to animals. With some effort and aggressive development of new biomedical research technologies, full replacement of animals in harmful research is within our grasp. The goal will not be reached all at once, however, and phasing out invasive research on all nonhuman primates should be the priority.

Approximately 70,000 nonhuman primates are used for research in the United States each year, according to the U.S. Department of Agriculture, and another 45,000 are held or bred for research. They include macaques, baboons, marmosets, and other monkeys, as well as some chimpanzees. Moreover, these numbers are increasing in the United States and

Canada. The rise is driven in part by the "high-fidelity" notion (supported by very little careful scientific justification) that primates are likely to be better models than mice and rats for studying human diseases, and partly by the sheer availability of primates.

The availability factor is a result of historical accident. In the 1960s, the United States invested in a significant infrastructure for primate research through creation of the National Primate Research Centers. The primate center program was the result of two unrelated occurrences. First, in the 1950s, hundreds of thousands of wild primates were captured and imported to support the race to develop a poliomyelitis vaccine. By 1960, with polio vaccines in use, this "race" was essentially over, but laboratories still had tens of thousands of primates. Then, they became swept up in another kind of race. The Russians had beaten the United States into space by launching the first satellite, creating panic that Russian science was outpacing U.S. science. American scientists made the argument that, because the Russians had a big primate research center, the United States should also have one or more primate centers. Seven facilities, formally recognized as government-supported institutions, were set up to provide support for and opportunities to do research in nonhuman primates.

Phasing out primate use should be a priority for ethical, scientific, and economic reasons.

The centers did not produce the hoped-for results. Three federal assessments found that the research conducted by the centers fell far short of expectations in terms of quality, and many deficiencies were also noted.[2] In the early 1980s, these centers were "rescued," in a sense, by the discovery that primates at the California Regional Primate Research Center were suffering from a simian version of AIDS. Suddenly, there was renewed focus on research in nonhuman primates. There are now eight National Primate Research Centers, the objective of which continues to be "to provide support for scientists who use NHPs in their research."[3]

Primates are used for a wide variety of research purposes. An analysis of one thousand federally funded studies that involved nonhuman primates found that research on HIV accounted for about 27 percent of the funding, followed by colony maintenance (likely because caring for primates is costly) at 15 percent, neurological research at 14 percent, and developmental research at 10 percent.[4]

Arguments for Phasing Out Primate Research

Phasing out primate use should be a priority for ethical, scientific, and economic reasons. The ethical concerns fall into two categories. One of them is the nature of the primates themselves. They are well known for their cognitive and emotional abilities. Studies demonstrate that they have mathematical, memory, and problem-solving skills and that they experience emotions similar to those of humans—for example, depression, anxiety, and joy. Chimpanzees can learn human languages, such as American Sign Language. Primates also have very long lifespans, which is an ethical issue because they are typically held in laboratories for decades and experimented on repeatedly. The other category of ethical concern is how primates are treated. Each year, thousands are captured from the wild, mostly in Asia and Mauritius, and transported to other countries. For example, China sets up breeding colonies, and the infants are sold to various countries, including the United States and European countries. The animals experience considerable stress, such as days of transport in small crates and restrictions on food and water intake. Studies show that it takes months for their physiological systems to return to baseline levels,[5] and then they face the trauma of research, including infection with virulent diseases, social isolation, food and water deprivation, withdrawal from drugs, and repeated surgeries.

Providing for the welfare of primates in a laboratory setting is very challenging. According to the Animal Welfare Act, each facility must develop and follow a plan for environmental enhancement to promote the psychological well-being of nonhuman primates. The plan must address social grouping; enriching the environment, with special consideration for great apes; caring for infants, young juveniles, and those primates showing signs of psychological distress; and ensuring the well-being of those primates who are used in a protocol requiring restricted activity.

Social companionship is the most important psychological factor for most primates. Federal law requires institutions to house primates in groups unless there is justification, such as debilitation as a result of age or other conditions, for housing them alone. But a recent analysis of documents from two large facilities obtained by The Humane Society of the United States demonstrates that primates spent an average of 53 percent of their lives housed alone. In many instances, a metal shape hung for a month on the bars of a metal cage was deemed to constitute adequate "enrichment."[6]

Much of the research with nonhuman primates is either of questionable value or has not been carefully evaluated and justified.

There have been only a few detailed examinations of the scientific value of primate use, and most were undertaken in Europe.[7] While there has been no general review of the usefulness of primate research in the United States, chimpanzee research has recently come in for very careful evaluation and serves as a case study for how all primate use should be examined. The Institute of Medicine's landmark 2011 report, *Chim-*

panzees in Biomedical and Behavioral Research: Assessing the Necessity, concluded that "most current use of chimpanzees for biomedical research is unnecessary."[8] (See "Raising the Bar: The Implications of the IOM Report on the Use of Chimpanzees in Research," in this volume [not included].) Most countries have banned research on chimpanzees, and there has been great pressure in Europe to end other primate use. A group chaired by Sir Patrick Bateson, current president of the Zoological Society of London and professor of animal behavior at Cambridge University, as well as former secretary of the Royal Society, published a report in 2011 that reviewed research using nonhuman primates in the United Kingdom. It is important to note that around 70 percent of all primate use in the United Kingdom is conducted to satisfy legislative or regulatory testing requirements and not necessarily because primates are essential for satisfying scientific goals.

The Bateson report recommended that all proposed primate studies be assessed using the following parameters: scientific value, probability of medical or other benefit, availability of alternatives, and likelihood and extent of animal suffering.[9] The report indicated that if a proposed use would cause severe suffering, it should be allowed only if there is a high likelihood of benefit. The report considered approximately 9 percent of the studies it examined to be of low importance and to inflict high levels of suffering.[10] The report was critical of some of the neuroscience research, which represented nearly half of the research surveyed. It found that half of the thirty-one neuroscience studies took a high toll on animal welfare, although most were also considered to be of high scientific value. Two of the studies were of concern because they posed a "high welfare impact," but moderate-quality science and little medical benefit.[11] The report recommended that more consideration be given to alternatives to nonhuman primates, including brain imaging, noninvasive electrophysiological technologies, in vitro and in silico techniques, and even research on human subjects.[12] The report recommended other ways of reducing the number of primates needed for research, including data sharing, publication of all results, and periodic review of outcomes, benefits, and impact of the research. "Researchers using NHPs have a moral obligation to publish results—even if negative—in order to prevent work from being repeated unnecessarily," the report states.[13]

> *The process that culminated in the phasing out of invasive research on chimpanzees in the United States in 2011 can and should be applied to all other nonhuman primates.*

In addition to the ethical and scientific arguments for ending research involving primates, there are economic reasons. Primates are very expensive to maintain. The eight National Primate Research Centers alone receive $1 billion of the National Institutes of Health's total $32 billion budget. The care and upkeep of primates other than chimpanzees is twenty to twenty-five dollars per day, compared with twenty cents to about $1.60 per day for small rodents. We argue that much of the research with nonhuman primates is either of questionable value or has not been carefully evaluated and justified. Therefore, these funds might be better spent on other research models, including several technologies that could replace nonhuman primates and other animals. Francis Collins, director of the NIH, argued in 2011 that new high-throughput approaches could overcome the drawbacks of animal models— they are slow, expensive, and not sufficiently relevant to human biology and pharmacology.[14]

Several such technologies are available. The U.S. Army recently announced that it would end the use of monkeys for chemical casualty training courses and replace them with alternatives such as simulators that mimic the effects of nerve gas on victims.[15]

Following Chimpanzees

The process that culminated in the phasing out of invasive research on chimpanzees in the United States in 2011 can and should be applied to all other nonhuman primates. Public opinion and ethical challenges drove that process. Even before the 2011 IOM report, scientists in the United States were having difficulty justifying why they should perform experiments on chimpanzees when their colleagues in other countries had stopped doing so. Unlike nonhuman primates in general, the number of chimpanzees in U.S. labs has been declining since reaching its peak in the late 1990s.

The main drivers for efforts to phase out research on chimpanzees are their genetic, biological, and behavioral similarities with humans.[16] Chimpanzees are humans' closest relative. Chimpanzee cognition has been studied extensively, and their capabilities are considerable. As with other primates, the impact of laboratory life—including barren housing and social isolation—on chimpanzees can last decades due to their long lifespan and thus raises significant welfare concerns. There is evidence that some chimpanzees used in research suffer from a form of posttraumatic stress disorder similar to that of humans. In their 2008 article, Gay Bradshaw and colleagues described the plight of a chimpanzee named Jeannie who endured invasive research and social isolation for over a decade. She exhibited abnormal behavior, including self-injury, bouts of aggression, and, according to laboratory documentation, a "nervous breakdown." When retired to a sanctuary, she recovered partially, but was ultimately diagnosed with complex PTSD. The paper concluded: "The costs of laboratory-caused trauma are immeasurable in their life-long psychological impact on, and consequent suffering of, chimpanzees."[17]

As we have done with chimpanzees, we need to critically analyze current uses of other nonhuman primates, the viability of alternative models, and the economic issues involved to forge the best way forward. A good starting point would be the formation of a working group of diverse stakeholders who agree that ending primate research is a worthwhile goal. Such a working group—possibly organized by the NIH and the National Academies—would analyze the necessity of primate use and identify existing and potential alternatives.

Now is the time for an internationally coordinated effort to define a strategy to replace all invasive research on primates.

The stakeholder group could develop a concrete plan to work on common-ground issues. This would involve developing priorities, short-term outcomes, and related activities. The ongoing Human Toxicology Project Consortium's work to ultimately replace all animals for toxicity testing is a good example of this approach. (See "No Animals Harmed: Toward a Paradigm Shift in Toxicity Testing," in this volume [not included].) The mission of the consortium is to "serve as a catalyst for the prompt, global, and coordinated implementation of '21st Century' toxicology, which will better safeguard human health and hasten the replacement of animal use in toxicology."[18] Because science is ever-changing, there must be an ongoing analysis of new technologies and challenges, and regulatory authorities must adjust regulations accordingly. In the United States, many stakeholders express frustration with the fact that the Food and Drug Administration, for example, favors data from outdated tests, including those that involve primates and other animals.

Phasing out invasive research on all nonhuman primates would take courage on the part of leaders in science and policy. It is a formidable task, but similarly transformative changes in how we conduct biomedical research have been achieved. At various points in the past century and a quarter, restrictions have been placed on particular kinds of human and animal research because of ethical issues, despite objections that such restrictions would slow scientific progress; think, for instance, of the Helsinki Declaration to protect human subjects in research and the animal welfare laws in the United States and the European Union. However, these laws have not slowed the pace of discovery about biology and disease processes. If anything, there has been an acceleration of such discovery in the half-century since these restrictions went into effect.

In the early 1950s, Sir Peter Medawar pressed the Universities Federation for Animal Welfare to develop a report on how laboratory animal welfare could be improved and how distress and suffering in the research laboratory might be reduced. That initiative led to publication of a volume on humane experimental approach that is now regarded as the foundation for the concept of the Three Rs of replacement, reduction, and refinement of animal studies.[19] Ten years later, in 1969, Medawar correctly predicted that laboratory animal use would peak within ten years and then start to decline. He argued that animal research would allow researchers to develop the knowledge and understanding that would lead, eventually, to the replacement of animal use in laboratories. In 2010, forty years after Medawar's prediction, laboratory animal use is approximately 50 percent of what it was in 1970. Francis Collins has pointed to the down sides of animal-based research—that is "time-consuming, costly, and may not accurately predict efficacy in humans."[20] He has also suggested that nonanimal technologies might be quicker and more effective in new drug discovery programs. Given the trends and political will, we believe that we could reach Medawar's prediction of complete replacement by 2050.

Now is the time for an internationally coordinated effort to define a strategy to replace all invasive research on primates. At the very least, we need to move quickly to reverse the increase in laboratory primate use in the United States and Canada. Until replacement is a realistic option, we must reduce the number of primates used and refine studies to reduce their suffering, for the sake of both animal welfare and science.

Notes

1. C. Blakemore, "Should We Experiment on Animals? Yes," *Telegraph*, October 28, 2008.

2. A.N. Rowan, *Of Mice, Models and Men* (Albany: State University of New York Press, 1984).

3. Department of Health and Human Services, Funding Opportunity for the National Primate Research Centers, http://grants.nih.gov/grants/guide/pa-files/PAR-11-136.html, accessed July 7, 2011.

4. K.M. Conlee, E.H. Hoffeld, and M.L. Stephens, "A Demographic Analysis of Primate Research in the United States," *Alternatives to Laboratory Animals* 32, suppl. 1A (2004): 315–22.

5. P.E. Honess, P.J. Johnson, and S.E. Wolfensohn, "A Study of Behavioural Responses of Non-Human Primates to Air Transport and Re-Housing," *Laboratory Animals* 38, no. 2 (2004): 119–32; J.M. Kagira et al., "Hematological Changes in Vervet Monkeys (*Chlorocedub aethiops*) during Eight Months' Adaptation to Captivity," *American Journal of Primatology* 69, no. 9 (2007): 1053–63.

6. J. Balcombe and K.M. Conlee, "Primate Life in Two American Laboratories," presentation to the Eighth World Congress on Alternatives and Animal Use in the Life Sciences, held in Montreal, Quebec, Canada, on August 21–25, 2011.

7. P. Bateson, *A Review of Research Using Nonhuman Primates: A Report of a Panel Chaired by Professor Sir Patrick Bateson, FRS* (London and Wiltshire, U.K.: Biotechnology and Biological Sciences Research Council, Medical Research Council, and Wellcome Trust, 2011) http://www.mrc.ac.uk/Utilities/Documentrecord/index.htm?d =MRC008083; J.A. Smith and K.M. Boyd, eds., *The Use of Non-Human Primates in Research and Testing* (Leicester, U.K.: British Psychological Society, 2002); D. Weatherall, *The Use of Non-Human Primates in Research: A Working Group Report Chaired by Sir David Weatherall FRS FmedSci* (London: Academy of Medical Sciences, 2006), http://www.acmedsci.ac.uk/images/project/nhpdownl.pdf.

8. Institute of Medicine, Committee on the Use of Chimpanzees in Biomedical and Behavioral Research, *Chimpanzees in Biomedical and Behavioral Research: Assessing the Necessity* (Washington, D.C.: National Academies Press, 2011), 4.

9. Bateson, *A Review of Research Using Nonhuman Primates*, 2.

10. Ibid., 1.

11. Ibid., 12–13.

12. Ibid., 4, 5, 16.

13. Ibid., 3.

14. F.S. Collins, "Reengineering Translational Science: The Time Is Right," *Science Translational Medicine* 3, no. 90 (2011): 1–6.

15. B. Vastag, "Army to Phase Out Animal Nerve-Agent Testing," *Washington Post*, October 13, 2011.

16. G.W. Bradshaw et al., "Building Inner Sanctuary: Complex PTSD in Chimpanzees," *Journal of Trauma and Dissociation* 9, no. 1 (2008): 9–34; J.A. Smith and K.M. Boyd, eds., *The Boyd Group Papers on the Use of Non-Human Primates in Research and Testing* (Leicester, U.K.: British Psychological Society, 2002).

17. Bradshaw et al., "Building Inner Sanctuary," 31.

18. Human Toxicology Project Consortium Web site, http://htpconsortium .wordpress.com/about-2, accessed February 13, 2012.

19. W.M.S. Russell and R.L. Burch, *The Principles of Humane Experimental Technique* (London: Methuen, 1959).

20. F.S. Collins, "Reengineering Translational Science," 3.

Vivisection Is Right, But It Is Nasty—And We Must Be Brave Enough to Admit This

Michael Hanlon

Michael Hanlon is a science journalist and author of numerous popular science books, including Eternity: Our Next Billion Years.

So, is it OK to sew kittens' eyelids together to stop children going blind? All too often the arguments surrounding live-animal experimentation, aka vivisection, circle around the putative torments of genetically engineered rodents (which no one much cares about) and monstrous cruelties inflicted on our ape close-cousins (illegal here anyway). But the story that scientists at Cardiff University have been studying the way brains react to induced blindness by 'modelling' the condition in young cats has crystallised the arguments in a way that may end up being very helpful.

The British Union for the Abolition of Vivisection says that raising newborn kittens in total darkness and sewing shut the eyes of others is not only cruel but unnecessary. Firstly they say it is possible to study the effects of lazy-eye, or Ambylopia, in human volunteers (not, presumably, involving eyelid stitching). Worse, they say, cat brains and cat vision are fundamentally different to ours and it is hard to see how anything useful can be gained by this research. These experiments have been done before, many years ago, and we still do not have a cure.

I have always believed animal experimentation is not only right but a moral necessity. Put simply, without the use of animals in the lab we would not have modern medicine. We would have no cancer drugs, no effective antibiotics, no proper analgesics. Many surgical procedures would be impossible. Of course medicine could advance on an ad hoc basis using only humans as guinea pigs but that would require us to live in a totally alien ethical (not to mention legal) world.

I have always decried the antics of the loonies, the people who put letter bombs and faeces through the front doors of scientists, the activists who make working at any lab involving animal experimentation an exercise akin to being a member of the RUC in 1970s Ulster. These people do their cause no good.

And one of the main arguments against animal-rights lunacy is the sheer hypocrisy. Last year, according to the Home Office, 3.8m 'procedures' were carried out on animals in Britain in the name of science and medicine. There is no doubt that although some pain and suffering was caused, most of these animal recruits lead better lives, and certainly better deaths, than the estimated billion or so chickens, bullocks, pigs and lambs slaughtered in the same period to provide us with food.

Animal experimentation is nasty. That does not make it wrong, but those of us who defend it must be brave enough to admit the truth, in all its grisly detail.

Any argument about animal welfare in the lab is specious in a nation which still allows battery poultry farming. And yet it is not quite so simple as that. Even carnivores can see, for instance, that (say) squirting makeup into the eyes of rabbits in the name of human vanity is wrong even if we are happy to throw said bunny in the pot with some onions and red wine. So what about injecting chemotherapy or AIDS drugs into the veins of the same rabbit to see what happens? Better than the cosmetic tests, for sure, but on a very emotional level something feels very different about messing around with an animal to make us (maybe, one day) feel better and simply killing it to satiate our meat-hunger (of course as far as the rabbit is concerned this is angels-on-pinhead stuff).

What would help is a bit more honesty. All too often scientists and doctors lapse into euphemism and obfuscation when describing procedures that must be unendurable in a small number of cases. They often talk about 'discomfort', when they mean 'screaming agony' for example (in fact too many doctors are prone to do this with human patients. If this is something that is taught in medical school, please can it be stopped, now).

Yesterday Cardiff University put out a press release defending the kitten business which failed to acknowledge or even mention the grisly nature of the procedure and certainly did not address the reality that as far as the animals were concerned this would have been hugely unpleasant. In a world where 1600 animals (the vast bulk being chickens) are slaughtered every second for food, most in conditions that do not bear thinking about, it does seem facile to be considering the 'rights' of 31 Welsh kittens stumbling around their pens in the dark.

Facile, perhaps but necessary too. The scientists are, generally, right about this; research like this is needed. But they need to be made to keep reminding us why it is right and to keep justifying procedures that, without the watchful eye of the BUAV (and, yes, the loonies as well) would perhaps become so routine that no one would give them a moment's thought. Animal experimentation is nasty. That does not make it wrong, but those of us who defend it must be brave enough to admit the truth, in all its grisly detail.

Primate Research Is Vital

Nicole Garbarini

Nicole Garbarini holds a PhD in biomedical sciences and is a writer and former reviews editor for Disease Models & Mechanisms.

When choosing a model organism to study disease and disease mechanisms, scientists rarely base their selection on basic biology alone. External influences such as the availability of collaborators, facilities and staff all factor into this decision, as do the personal preferences of the investigator. Several, small, cost-effective animal models are available that can provide robust and meaningful data that are relevant to human disease phenomena. Organisms with short reproductive cycles, a rapid turnover of generations, and exquisite genetic tractability can rapidly provide statistically significant results. However, one animal model that has absolutely none of these qualities remains a mainstay in human disease research: the non-human primate. Working with non-human primates not only presents many technical challenges, but also unique financial and ethical challenges. Weighing these unique challenges against the benefits for human disease research presents a paradox for scientists and research institutions: whether to embrace, or abandon, primate research. However, several aspects of primate biology keep researchers persevering through financial and political challenges.

Research Under Pressure

All animal research receives some level of criticism from animal rights advocates, with protests escalating the further one climbs the phylogenetic or evolutionary tree. However, in the last few years, heightened threats and assaults from animal rights activists have waged a war between 'primate liberation' groups and the scientists who perform primate research. In 2007 and 2008, acts of violence against non-human primate researchers most notably included a string of attacks on UCLA (University of California, Los Angeles) and UC (University of California) Santa Cruz professors, who were targeted at their homes with fire-starting devices and other threatening actions and materials. In the wake of such incidents, the scientific community has increasingly responded to the mounting attacks on scientists and their families, calling for an end to the violence and for increased protection.

Other animal rights supporters have taken non-criminal and legislatively savvy methods of fighting against primate research. For example, in the USA, the well-known animal rights group PETA (People for the Ethical Treatment of Animals), which opposes all medical research on animals, offers clerkships in animal law—a law specialty that is now taught in many law schools worldwide. PETA hires undercover investigators to work in medical research labs and record lab experiments through journals, photographs and videos in order to expose 'the shocking reality of animal suffering,' and to find violations of animal care protocols. One such investigation at the Oregon National Primate Research Center gathered enough evidence to result in a United States Department of Agriculture (USDA)-led investigation and an official USDA warning against the facility.

High expectations are set for primate care, and most universities want facilities that go above and beyond the minimum care requirements.

Many signs point to the fact that such pressures, combined, have been effectively influencing researchers, research institutions and legislators to limit primate research. In the

USA, Indiana University, which only had two primate labs but boasts a robust medical research program, ended all primate research campus-wide in 2008. In an e-mail interview, researcher Preston Garraghty stated, 'The decision here destroyed my research career on this campus.' Garraghty's work on synaptic plasticity, learning and memory uses squirrel monkeys as a model system. 'The President of this institution, in rendering his unilateral decision, encouraged me to find an alternative model system,' Garraghty stated. 'That's like asking a developmental psychologist interested in, say, child language acquisition, to use song birds. The President's ignorance, naiveté and stupidity is astounding.' As a well-established researcher, Garraghty describes switching models in the late stage of his career as 'verging on impossible.' 'It is hard enough to secure external funding to support research for which one is well known,' Garraghty said, and he plans on continuing his research through collaborations at other universities.

In Europe, limits on non-human primate research have been continually contested in government. In late 2008, European Parliament draft legislation proposed new restrictions that scientists say would effectively ban most non-human primate studies. However, in May 2009, the directive was revised to allow greater flexibility for researchers, in that basic science research can be performed on monkeys, and not just studies of 'life-threatening' disease.

High Costs

Another pressure facing primate research is the cost of animal care. In an interview with Jon Kaas, a Vanderbilt University researcher, Kaas describes primate research as not inherently more costly than rat or mouse research, since primate researchers keep relatively few individual animals because fewer animals are usually used in experiments. However, high expectations are set for primate care, and most universities want facilities that go above and beyond the minimum care requirements. For example, primate centers have vastly increased their staff, including full-time vets and enrichment officers/coordinators (to make sure that primates get adequate socialization and stimulation). Kaas notes that primate facilities employ five times more staff members than a decade ago. Although official regulations have not changed much, the perceived requirements are for an increasingly higher standard of facility. Asked about why universities may be increasingly critical of facility conditions, Kaas suggests that this increased attention helps to prevent any devastating interruptions in research. '[Universities want] to prevent any mistakes or violations so that the institution won't receive a severe fine or, at the worst case, suspend all research. Research is a multimillion dollar enterprise for a university.'

Researchers continue to perform research on non-human primates because, as model organisms for studying disease, non-human primates provide unique insights that cannot be studied in lower-order organisms.

Kathy Grant, a researcher at the Oregon National Primate Research Center, whose own research career has utilized both primates and rodents, echoes this sentiment. 'I think a lot of universities now do look at their research portfolio and wonder at what level is this research no longer viable, if you will, from the financial point of view,' Grant noted. She also adds that animal rights is a big issue for public relations of colleges and universities, given how it may affect financial contributions and public opinion. 'There is concern as to whether or not alumni associations are comfortable or not with particular research programs. This isn't only about monkey research but other potentially controversial science, such as stem cell research, too.'

Likewise, Kaas notes that activist interference with research can add to the cost of primate research, both in terms of money and time. 'For a tenured professor, it might not matter as much since he/she won't lose his/her job, but for a younger faculty member who is just getting started, interruptions in research can result in not getting tenure.' Citing the case of a colleague in Iowa, he noted that, if such a situation affects the research of an investigator towards the start of their career, some institutions would give an extension of time before tenure review.

Reasons to Continue Using Primates as Animal Models

Regardless of political and financial pressures, researchers continue to perform research on non-human primates because, as model organisms for studying disease, non-human primates provide unique insights that cannot be studied in lower-order organisms. Additionally, non-human primates offer opportunities for disease research that cannot be provided by examining disease in humans. Several areas of medicine benefit from non-human primate research, and range from cardiovascular and metabolic disease to infectious diseases, autoimmune disease or pulmonary disorders.

The field of neuroscience is one such area of biomedical research that utilizes non-human primates for both basic science research as well as disease research. Intelligence, cognition and emotion—the same characteristics that raise ethical concerns for primate research—are the same faculties that are destroyed in some of the most puzzling diseases of our time, such as Alzheimer's disease, and drug and alcohol addiction.

Marina Emborg, Assistant Professor of Medical Physics at the University of Wisconsin-Madison, co-authored a 2008 *Lancet* article discussing the contributions of non-human primates to translational and basic science research in neuroscience. Emborg and her co-author, John P. Capitanio, describe how non-human primate studies help advance basic disease pathology studies. Primate studies have had an important role in the development of clinical treatments, such as stem cell and gene transfer therapies, before Phase I patient trials. Additionally, Emborg and Capitanio cite studies on primates that have contributed to understanding neurobehavioral outcomes that result from gene-environment interactions. The authors focus on Parkinson's disease, Alzheimer's disease, neuroAIDS and stress-related disease as key neurobiological illnesses that have benefited from primate research.

Emborg's own work focuses on modeling Parkinson's disease in aged monkeys. In an interview, Emborg added that neurotoxin models of Parkinson's disease have contributed greatly to the development of therapies for humans. Deep brain stimulation, for instance, was tested on animals that were administered the drug MPTP, which causes parkinsonian symptoms in both animals and humans.

In studying alcohol abuse, . . . the differences between rodents and primates are large enough to necessitate using non-human primates to accurately study human drinking behaviors.

'One reason that we use primates is because their behavior is much more complex, so the answers we are going to find are much closer than those we will find in humans,' Emborg notes. She also describes how the bigger volume of primate brains, as well as the complexity of their brain structures, is another key factor that supports the use of primates as model organisms, particularly when studying the basal ganglia, which are the structures that are affected by Parkinson's disease. 'In the human or monkey, the caudate and putamen are well delineated and separated by the internal capsule. If you look into the brain of a rodent, the clear delineation is not there. When you are testing therapies, for instance using stem cell transplants or gene therapy as an example, you have to take into account the volume of the space, as well as the internal capsule, as it might prevent you from administering the therapeutic molecules or cells in one injection. In primates and humans, you will probably have to target the caudate and putamen separately.'

Addiction Research

Kathy Grant has been using several different animal models throughout her research career to study the brain and behavior in regard to addiction disorders. Her graduate school research utilized rat models of alcoholism, and her postdoctoral work at the University of Chicago used monkeys to study drug abuse. From there, she has been at several different private and government institutions researching, and consulting on using, mice, rats and monkeys as disease models. Her current work focuses on behavioral pharmacology; drug and alcohol abuse; and addiction studies. Now located at the Oregon National Primate Research Center, she not only works with monkeys, but also has a rat and mouse lab as well.

'The animal that I use is dependent on the question that I'm asking,' says Grant. 'I consider which species is going to give me the best answer to the question that I am investigating.'

In studying alcohol abuse, she says that the differences between rodents and primates are large enough to necessitate using non-human primates to accurately study human drinking behaviors. 'The amount of alcohol consumed by some individual monkeys rivals the amount that human alcoholics will drink, and we have trouble showing that kind of intake in mice and rats. You can show it, but you have to take measures such as selectively breeding for high alcohol preference, depriving the rodents of food, making them dependent on alcohol over repeated cycles, and increase intake over time,' says Grant. 'The topography of being able to gulp down your drinks might be one signature of a primate. We can fill our buccal cavities with a lot of fluid and swallow it right down, whereas rodents are like dogs in that they lap at water to drink.'

A large part of Grant's work involves interactions between alcohol and the endocrine and reproductive systems, for instance in investigating fetal alcohol syndrome. Her work also examines the impact of drinking or abusing alcohol at different stages at life, for example, while children and teenagers are developing through puberty. The high similarity between humans and primates is a key component to these studies, not only because of the neurological correlates, but also because of the similarity between hypothalamic-pituitary-adrenal (HPA) axis responses, and menstruation and pregnancy. The fact that the longevity of non-human primates is comparable to humans is also important.

Using primates allows researchers to investigate the true risk of alcoholic drinking and drinking during pregnancy.

'Neurosteroids are really important in sleep regulation, and we know that sleep is really dysregulated with drinking [alcohol], especially heavy drinking,' says Grant. 'We also know [sleep] remains dysregulated even when the alcoholic or alcohol abuser is abstinent, and that it is one of the more prolonged withdrawal symptoms. So this is a whole area of research where [scientists] would want an animal model that is long-lived.'

Humans Aren't Usable

When asked why human epidemiological studies were not feasible for this work, Grant used examples from the alcohol field to discuss the types of problems that are commonly encountered when studying substance abuse in human subjects.

'Humans are really, really lousy at being accurate about telling you how much they had to drink. That could be because they don't remember, because it's in a social setting and there are many things going on and they just don't know, or because they are trying to hide their drinking. They may even be in trouble with the law and trying not to drink, so there are a lot of reasons why humans are not accurate,' said Grant. '[Using primates,] we know exactly how much these animals not only drank yesterday, but also last week and last year. We know exactly what their nutritional status is, which is another really difficult thing to track in humans. Also, human alcoholics have a high comorbidity with smoking. Trying to separate the effects of alcohol in studying markers like cognitive performance, and to separate out other factors like cancer, is very difficult.' Furthermore, using primates allows researchers to investigate the true risk of alcoholic drinking and drinking during pregnancy. 'In addressing the question of adolescent drinking leading to a four times, lifelong higher risk of being diagnosed with alcohol abuse or alcoholism, we can't randomize these subjects because it is ethically wrong.' Grant also cited the issue of self-selection in human studies. 'A Wayne State study carried out about 20 years ago says that if a woman stops drinking in her third trimester, there will be a better outcome for her child. Again, this isn't randomized. We want to know what the factors are that determines who can stop drinking before the third trimester, and who cannot.'

In discussing the larger impact of these studies, beyond simply learning about the biology of disease, Grant commented, 'All of this we do, is not just because we want to know, but it is so that we can have accurate public health information out there about what is safe and not safe.'

Spinal Cord Research

Jon Kaas at Vanderbilt University is participating in studies of spinal cord injury using primate models. He points out that some studies can utilize rats and mice first, in the early stages of research, but comments, 'Rats won't get us where we need to be in order to understand spinal cord injury in patients.' One key difference in the spinal cord connections is that, unlike in primates, the pyramidal tract, which conducts motor control, and the ascending sensory pathway, which relays sensory information to the brain, are mixed in rats, so you cannot study these pathways in isolation of one another.

We are doing human studies, but we realized that there are a lot of basic questions that we can't address either in a mouse model or by doing studies in humans.

Another difference that Kaas notes is detectable on a very macroscopic level, 'Rats don't have hands.' Since his spinal cord injury research includes analysis of hand control, using primates is crucial to determine whether axon regeneration is sufficient to establish hand movements, or whether a brain-directed hand or arm prosthesis will work. Small improvements in movement make a large impact for some spinal cord injury patients. 'Working with the Christopher Reeve Foundation, you see people with different levels of spinal cord injury. Even if [quadriplegic] patients can get a little bit more hand movement, they can do most jobs,' Kaas explained. 'Regaining executive use of the hands and arms is a big accomplishment, allowing patients to do desk jobs, work at computers, and get where they need to go using a wheelchair, which is better than only being able to use/move their mouths. Even if they can get a little bit of recovery, it will make a huge difference in their lives.'

Reproductive biology is another research area with compelling reasons to use primates for human disease studies. Significant differences exist between primate and rodent reproductive biology, as well as between primates and larger animals that are used in the laboratory, such as dogs and pigs. Many of the key differences revolve around the female reproductive system, including organ shape, the length of gestation, ovulation cycles, and the number of live births (litters versus individuals). In addition, there are many human diseases that are specific to the female reproductive system, such as ovarian cancer. Furthermore, much research revolves around identifying environmental factors that affect oocyte development, or that affect the fetus during gestation.

'I always said that I would never work with anything higher [in the phylogenetic tree] than a mouse,' says Pat Hunt, a researcher of reproductive biology at Washington State University in the USA. Throughout her research career, Hunt combined human studies with mouse model work in order to study oocyte development and genetic quality, specifically the chromosomal changes that occur with advanced maternal age and that lead to an increased incidence of developmental abnormalities. A few years ago, her work took an unexpected twist when her mice were inadvertently exposed to a chemical leaching from newly acquired water bottles. The estrogen-like chemical, bisphenol A (BPA), started to cause abnormalities in the mice—a particularly concerning effect, considering the prevalence of BPA in food and drink packaging such as baby bottles, water bottles, and the interior coating of food and beverage cans.

I think these studies are really important and need to be done, otherwise I wouldn't undertake them.

From this initial observation, Hunt began to pursue a number of different studies to understand the influence of BPA on the reproductive system. 'Everything we do convinces me that this chemical is something we need to be concerned about,' Hunt says. Although she found that the mouse was an excellent model in many respects, she found herself at a critical point where, in order to emphasize the impact of BPA on human health, she would need to expand her studies to other systems. 'We are doing human studies, but we realized that there are a lot of basic questions that we can't address either in a mouse model or by doing studies in humans.'

Hunt explained that such basic questions include understanding how BPA is metabolized, and what specific dosages damage the oocytes. Early data suggest that humans metabolize BPA differently than mice, and that pregnant individuals may metabolize BPA differently compared with non-pregnant individuals. Also, the fundamental differences in the reproductive systems of primates versus mice may influence how BPA affects oocytes, since mice are litter-bearing animals, ovulate multiple eggs at once, and can experience pseudopregnancy.

Some corollary studies have been performed to compare maternal serum BPA levels, and the effects on fetal tissues. However, Hunt points out that these studies only provide a small snapshot of the issue, when in fact it is likely to be a lifelong chemical accumulation process. Since BPA is widely present, it is difficult to calculate chemical exposure based on self-reporting. Additionally, since oocytes are generated during fetal development, it is difficult to directly assess the influence of BPA exposure on oocyte defects because the effect of BPA exposure during fetal development can only be assessed after the subject reaches sexual maturity.

Thus, Hunt is working with colleagues in primate research centers to look at the effects of BPA in rhesus monkeys; different chemical dosages and periods of exposure; exposure during different stages of life; and to study the effects of BPA on the developing ovary and oocytes.

Hunt asserts that this type of research is necessary for commanding serious attention to BPA toxicity. 'We think [mice are] an excellent model in many respects, but critics say that these are only mice, and that we have no evidence that [humans] would respond the same way,' said Hunt. 'I think these studies are really important and need to be done, otherwise I wouldn't undertake them.'

Primate Research Technology Moves Ahead

In addition to these inherent biological factors that encourage work in non-human primates, primate animal models are also gaining advantages that formerly only worms, flies and mice could boast. Research on the genetic manipulation of primates continues to advance, demonstrating their potential for genetic tractability in order to model human disease.

In May 2008, Anthony Chan and colleagues at the Yerkes National Primate Research Center in Atlanta, GA, reported another exciting advance toward creating a more human-like animal model of disease. Their paper, published in *Nature*, describes the creation of transgenic monkeys as a model for Huntington's disease, a severe neurodegenerative disorder that is characterized by symptoms such as motor disturbances and cognitive decline. The report describing the first non-human transgenic primate was published in *Science* in 2001. Chan was also a member of this research group, led by Gerald Schatten, which successfully generated a transgenic monkey (named 'ANDi,' a reversed abbreviation of 'inserted DNA') carrying a green fluorescent protein reporter gene. This initial demonstration of technical ability, and the Huntington's disease model monkeys that were reported in 2008, are the only reports of transgenic non-human primates during the last 7 years. Although it is clear that these are major accomplishments, it is also clear that there are several limitations in the generation of transgenic primates.

In an interview, Chan said that one such factor is the limits on resources. Monkeys require more space and a more enriched environment than rodents, so housing and daily expenses add to the cost. He also noted that coordination with people and facilities can be 'very demanding.'

Chan's group has worked on optimizing techniques to reduce the number of animals used in his research. The initial work that produced ANDi used retroviral vectors for gene insertion, but this newer study used lentiviral vectors that, Chan says, produce close to 100% transgenic offspring. 'With that efficiency, the number of animals involved will be minimized. That's very important to reduce the number of animals and the cost.'

Other limiting factors include finding a surrogate female. Rather than using hormonal synchronization, which may further lessen the chance of a successful pregnancy, the hormonal cycles of females are monitored individually to find a surrogate when transgenic embryos are ready for transfer. 'Sometimes we have embryos that are ready, but we don't have a matching surrogate,' Chan described, 'we are not just dealing with the technique, but also the physiology of the animals.'

Other researchers are working on new techniques to help make transgenic animal generation more efficient, in terms of both speed and cost.

In describing precise time differences between mouse and primate reproductive cycles, Chan describes, '[monkeys] don't reach puberty in 4 weeks, they reach puberty in 3 to 4 years, and the gestation time is 150 to 160 days instead of 21 days [as in the mouse]. These are factors that we cannot change; instead we look for other ways to accelerate the process.'

One such method that Chan's group uses is in vitro fertilization and he noted that, in the future, sperm and eggs from transgenic monkeys can be harvested for assisted reproductive techniques, which will also help to speed up the generation of new transgenic animals for continued research.

Similarly, other researchers are working on new techniques to help make transgenic animal generation more efficient, in terms of both speed and cost. For example, Subeer Majumdar of the National Institute of Immunology in New Delhi, India, studies disease and reproduction in primates, and is developing new methods of transgene insertion with the ultimate goal of using such technology in primate models of human disease.

Majumdar explains that using the same approach in monkeys and mice does not take into account the differences in oocyte production between these animals. In mice, he ex-

plains, one sacrificed female mouse can provide up to 30 oocytes, so merely ten mice can provide the 200–300 oocytes
that are needed to begin an experiment. From here, approximately 40 to 50 survive pronuclear injection with the transgenic construct, and even fewer zygotes implant successfully in
the surrogate female. Furthermore, only a subset of the mouse
pups born will be transgenic.

In monkeys, however, Majumdar explains that the oocyte
harvesting method is very different. Anesthetized female monkeys are subject to survival surgeries using laproscopic techniques. Only four or five oocytes are available for retrieval,
and not all of them survive. Considering the post-injection
survival rate in mouse oocytes, Majumdar estimates that up to
80 animals may be needed to generate a starting pool of 300
oocytes.

---

*Young researchers will have to weigh the costs between
the scientific benefits of using non-human primate models and the issues of time, money, ethics and societal
pressures.*

In order to switch the odds in their favor, Majumdar and
colleagues are investigating ways to use males to carry the
transgene, rather than injecting DNA into an embryo. His
team published a paper in *Nature Methods* describing how
they introduce the transgenic construct into the testicular
stem cells of anesthetized male mice using electroporation of
the testes. Stem cells that successfully take up the transgene
produce sperm cells that contain the DNA construct. Majumdar commented that this technique takes less time, does not
involve sacrificing any animals, and involves fewer animals because there is no need for a surrogate female. 'Besides the
electroporation, the rest of the procedure is natural,' Majumdar commented, 'the mice mate naturally and there is no sur-

rogate mother. The female naturally produces babies, so there is only one place where you interfere—during the insertion of the gene.'

For these reasons, Majumdar sees this new method as very advantageous for making transgenic primates, because it might circumvent the limiting factors that make them difficult to produce. Chan agrees that the result 'sounds promising,' also adding, 'I think it'll be great if it works, but in the meantime we are focusing on the technology that we have in hand, which we believe will be more reliable.'

The Road Ahead

The future of primate research is moving forward, with new tools to enhance genetic tractability. However, the use of primates in medical research remains a hotly contested issue. Besides the ethics of this research, justifying the costs for staff and enhanced animal care will be important when competing for funding in a tight economy.

Young researchers will have to weigh the costs between the scientific benefits of using non-human primate models and the issues of time, money, ethics and societal pressures. In discussing the careers of trainees who have left his lab, Kaas says that he does see young scientists quit, or become intimidated. Some researchers from his lab never perform research in non-human primates, but prefer to switch to mouse or rat studies. Others do extended postdocs or fellowships to remain in primate research. And even more, Kaas notes with a laugh, scientists are taking another alternative to essentially stay in primate research—by working with humans. 'Fewer places are doing [non-human] primate research, but more places are doing research on humans through imaging centers, because there are facilities for that everywhere.'

CHAPTER 2

Does Factory Farming Violate Animal Rights?

Chapter Preface

Activists often argue against factory farming on the grounds that animals are kept in inhumane and cruel conditions. However, another criticism of factory farms concerns the issue of health. In particular, many experts argue that the widespread use of antibiotics in factory farming poses a threat to humans and may lead to drug-resistant diseases.

Animals in large-scale farms are routinely doused with antibiotics. Critics say this is done because the animals are kept in unhealthy and crowded conditions, and that the antibiotics are necessary to keep the animals from becoming sick with infections. Thus, the argument goes, the use of antibiotics is itself a sign that the animals are living in unsanitary conditions. Farmers, however, often point out that the antibiotics make the animals grow faster, and that they are not necessarily used because their environment is unhealthy.

In any case, critics fear that this wide-scale, everyday use of antibiotics can lead to bacteria developing immunity and resistance to common antibiotics. Alexander Zaitchik, writing in *Salon*, points to an incident in which four hundred people became sick with an antibiotic-resistant strain of salmonella after eating chickens raised in a factory farm in California. Zaitchik quotes Johns Hopkins environmental health science professor Robert Lawrence, who warned, "This is just the latest example of the enormity of the problem.... If we don't do something, we'll find ourselves back in the era where young people died of pneumonia. Industrial farming has created a perfect storm."[1]

Historian and author Maureen Ogle, however, questions whether factory farms cause the kind of dangerous antibiotic

---

1. Quoted in Alexander Zaitchik "Big Ag's Big Lie: Factory Farms, Your Health and the New Politics of Antibiotics," *Salon*, January 12, 2014. http://www.salon.com/2014/01/12/big_ags_big_lie_factory_farms_your_health_and_the_new_politics_of_antibiotics.

resistance that Lawrence predicts. Ogle points out that there is a lot of debate about whether using antibiotics is a good practice, but that there is no clear consensus on whether there is a definite link between the use of antibiotics on farms and the growth of antibiotic resistance. She says that "much of the resistance to antibiotics is showing up in so-called third world countries, where people rarely eat meat, let alone meat from animals raised on antibiotics."[2]

The remainder of this chapter looks at other issues surrounding factory farming, particularly about whether modern farming practices—or any animal farming practices—can be humane and consistent with animal rights.

2. Maureen Ogle, "'Attention Shoppers': A New Line of Attack Against Antibiotics on the Farm (Plus a Little History, of Course!)," June 21, 2012. http://www.maureen ogle.com/maureen-ogle/2012/06/21/attention-shoppers-a-new-line-of-attack-against -antibiotics-on-the-farm-plus-a-little-history-of-course?rq=Attention%20Shoppers.

Factory Farming of Chickens Is Cruel and Inhumane

Dawne McCance

Dawne McCance is distinguished professor of religion at the University of Manitoba.

Factory farming turned first to chickens and the industrialization of egg production. Whereas on traditional family farms, chickens usually ran free in barnyards, lived off the land by foraging, expressed their natural behaviors of moving freely, nest-building, dust-bathing, escaping from more aggressive animals, defecating away from their nests, and in general, "fulfilling their natures as chickens" [according to Bernard Rollin], the situation they experience on factory farms is vastly different—and well-documented and described in animal studies literature and on animal welfare websites. Once hatched in industrial breeding houses, female egg-laying chicks are separated from males. They do not lay eggs, and because their flesh is of poor quality, male chicks "are, literally, thrown away. We watched at one hatchery as 'chick-pullers' weeded males from each tray and dropped them into heavy-duty plastic bags. Our guide explained: 'we put them in a bag and let them suffocate. A mink farmer picks them up and feeds them to his mink'" [according to Jim Mason and Peter Singer]. In *Animal Liberation*, [Peter] Singer notes that some male chicks "are ground up, while still alive, to be turned into food for their sisters. At least 160 million birds are gassed, suffocated, or die this way every year in the United States alone. Just how many suffer each particular fate is impossible to tell, because no records are kept: the growers think of getting rid of male chicks as we think of putting out the trash."

Dawne McCance, *Critical Animal Studies: An Introduction*. Albany, NY: State University of New York Press, 2013, pp. 10–12. Copyright © 2013 by State University of New York. All rights reserved. Reproduced by permission.

Inhumane Confinement

Female chicks are transferred to huge layer houses into which thousands of birds are crowded. The birds are confined in small wire cages that are often stacked in layers, each cage holding up to six or eight hens at a time, standing on top of each other with no room for any of them to stretch their wings. Laying hens spend their entire lives in these battery cages, incurring various foot and body injuries from the unforgiving wire floor and walls, defecating through the mesh to a collecting trench below, their food and water delivered by one conveyer system, their eggs collected by another. Because, when confined to so small a space they cannot establish a dominance hierarchy or pecking order, the birds are routinely "debeaked," to prevent their cannibalizing of each other. In *Animal Liberation*, Singer notes that the practice of debeaking began in San Diego in the 1940s, and used to be performed with a blow-torch, the farmer literally burning off the upper beaks of the chickens. "A modified soldering iron soon replaced this crude technique, and today specially designed guillotinelike devices with hot blades are the preferred instrument. The infant chick's beak is inserted into the instrument, and the hot blade cuts off the end of it. The procedure is carried out quickly, about fifteen birds a minute. Such haste means that the temperature and sharpness of the blade can vary, resulting in sloppy cutting and serious injury to the bird." In animal philosopher Bernard Rollin's words, "The animal is now an inexpensive cog in a machine, part of a factory, and the cheapest part at that, and thus totally expendable." Factory-farmed hens are raised to overproduce eggs. But at the age of about a year and a half, when their ability to produce eggs diminishes due to the wear and tear of cage life, and when it is no longer profitable to house and feed them, "they are made into soup and other processed foods" [according to Jim Mason and Peter Singer].

The Highest Yield

Chickens raised for meat, both males and females, once de-beaked, are housed in huge broiler buildings where they are raised, for a mere seven or eight weeks of life, not necessarily in cages, but still in intensely crowded, unnatural, dimly lighted, poorly ventilated, and ammonia-filled conditions that allow each bird less than a square foot of space. As Singer points out in *Animal Liberation*, aside from stress and threat of suffocation, chickens raised in such broiler houses face many disease and health hazards, including sudden or "acute death syndrome," ulcerated feet, crippling and deformities, lung damage from inhalation of dust and ammonia, breast blisters, and hock burns. Like layer hens, factory-made broilers never see the light of day—at least until they are ushered from the semidarkness of the broiler building, loaded into crates, and piled into the back of a truck to be driven to a processing plant for slaughter. Such intense aggregation of birds in confinement conditions typifies the density that is characteristic of factory farming overall, and that is designed to produce the highest possible yield at the lowest possible cost. Understandably, under such conditions, antibiotics are regularly used to prevent costly disease outbreaks. Singer asks whether, once factory broilers are hung upside down and killed, plucked, dressed, and sold to millions of families who gnaw on their bones, people pause "for an instant to think that they are eating the dead body of a once living creature, or to ask what was done to that creature in order to enable them to buy and eat its body."

Factory Farming Is Not the Only Way to Feed the World

Tom Philpott

Tom Philpott is a former food writer for Grist *and a writer for* Mother Jones *magazine.*

To "feed the world" by 2050, we'll need a massive, global ramp-up of industrial-scale, corporate-led agriculture. At least that's the conventional wisdom.

Against Big Ag

Even progressive journalists trumpet the idea.... The public-radio show Marketplace reported it as fact last week, earning a knuckle rap from Tom Laskway. At least one major strain of President Obama's (rather inconsistent) agricultural policy is predicated on it. And surely most agricultural scientists and development specialists toe that line . . . right?

Well, not really. Back in 2009, *Seed Magazine* organized a forum predicated on the idea that a "scientific consensus," analogous to the one on climate change, had formed around the desirability of patent-protected genetically modified seeds. If I must say so, my own contribution to that discussion shredded that notion. If anything, a pro-GMO consensus has formed among a narrow group of microbiologists—the people who conduct gene manipulations to develop novel crops. But no such accord exists among scientists whose work takes them out of the laboratory and into farm fields and ecosystems: soil experts, ecologists, development specialists, etc.

The latest evidence against any consensus around Big Ag as world savior: In a paper . . . just published in *Science*, a team of researchers led by the eminent Washington State University soil scientist John P. Reganold urges a fundamental rethinking of the U.S. ag-research system, which is "narrowly focused on productivity and efficiency" at the expense of public health and ecological resilience; and of the Farm Bill, which uses subsidies not to support a broad range of farmers but rather to "mask market, social, and environmental factors associated with conventional production systems."

The Reganold team's *Science* article distills their much longer report published last year by the prestigious National Research Council. While conventional wisdom holds that scientists who study agriculture think only lots of GMOs and agrichemicals can feed us going forward, Reganold's team has quite a different set of recommendations in mind: "organic farming, alternative livestock production (e.g., grass-fed), mixed crop and livestock systems, and perennial grains."

As far back as 2008, the largest-ever assessment of attitudes within the scientific community came out squarely against industrial agriculture as the true and only way to "feed the world" going forward.

They are by no means the only high-level researchers to reach such conclusions. Earlier this year, the U.N.'s special rapporteur on food, Olivier De Schutter, conducted "an extensive review of the recent scientific literature" and concluded that the case for Big Ag had been way overblown. Defying agrichemical industry dogma about how organic agriculture produces low yields, De Schutter declared, "Small-scale farmers can double food production within 10 years in critical regions by using ecological methods."

Also this spring, another branch of the United Nations, the U.N. Environment Program, released yet another report making the case for organic and other low-input ag techniques. . . .

The Debate

And as far back as 2008, the largest-ever assessment of attitudes within the scientific community came out squarely against industrial agriculture as the true and only way to "feed the world" going forward. The International Assessment of Agricultural Knowledge, Science, and Technology for Development (IAASTD), a three-year study released in 2008, engaged 400 scientists from around the globe under the aegis of the World Bank and the U.N.'s Food and Agriculture Organization. Far from pinning hopes for humanity's future on the products of a few agrichemical firms, the IAASTD focuses on building resilience and health in communities through sustainable-ag techniques it groups under the rubric of the term "agroecology."

Now, I would never insist that there is a consensus among scientists that only organic ag can feed the world. There are clearly scientists, not all of them linked financially to the agrichemical industry, who would passionately argue against that proposition. But there is by no means a consensus in the other direction. What we have is a *debate*—one being snuffed out by the illusion of a consensus. As global population grows and climate change proceeds apace, making agriculture ever more tricky, food policy may well emerge as *the* question of our time. It's time to air out that debate.

The Omnivore's Delusion: Against the Agri-Intellectuals

Blake Hurst

Blake Hurst is a farmer in Missouri.

I'm dozing, as I often do on airplanes, but the guy behind me has been broadcasting nonstop for nearly three hours. I finally admit defeat and start some serious eavesdropping. He's talking about food, damning farming, particularly livestock farming, compensating for his lack of knowledge with volume.

I'm so tired of people who wouldn't visit a doctor who used a stethoscope instead of an MRI demanding that farmers like me use 1930s technology to raise food. Farming has always been messy and painful, and bloody and dirty. It still is.

But now we have to listen to self-appointed experts on airplanes frightening their seatmates about the profession I have practiced for more than 30 years. I'd had enough. I turned around and politely told the lecturer that he ought not believe everything he reads. He quieted and asked me what kind of farming I do. I told him, and when he asked if I used organic farming, I said no, and left it at that. I didn't answer with the first thought that came to mind, which is simply this: I deal in the real world, not superstitions, and unless the consumer absolutely forces my hand, I am about as likely to adopt organic methods as the Wall Street Journal is to publish their next edition by setting the type by hand.

He was a businessman, and I'm sure spends his days with spreadsheets, projections, and marketing studies. He hasn't used a slide rule in his career and wouldn't make projections with tea leaves or soothsayers. He does not blame witchcraft for a bad quarter, or expect the factory that makes his product to use steam power instead of electricity, or horses and wagons to deliver his products instead of trucks and trains. But he expects me to farm like my grandfather, and not incidentally, I suppose, to live like him as well. He thinks farmers are too stupid to farm sustainably, too cruel to treat their animals well, and too careless to worry about their communities, their health, and their families. I would not presume to criticize his car, or the size of his house, or the way he runs his business. But he is an expert about me, on the strength of one book, and is sharing that expertise with captive audiences every time he gets the chance. Enough, enough, enough.

The combination of herbicides and genetically modified seed has made my farm more sustainable, not less, and actually reduces the pollution I send down the river.

Industrial Farming and Its Critics

Critics of "industrial farming" spend most of their time concerned with the processes by which food is raised. This is because the results of organic production are so, well, troublesome. With the subtraction of every "unnatural" additive, molds, fungus, and bugs increase. Since it is difficult to sell a religion with so many readily quantifiable bad results, the trusty family farmer has to be thrown into the breach, saving the whole organic movement by his saintly presence, chewing on his straw, plodding along, at one with his environment, his community, his neighborhood. Except that some of the largest farms in the country are organic—and are giant organizations dependent upon lots of hired stoop labor doing the most backbreaking of tasks in order to save the sensitive conscience of my fellow passenger the merest whiff of pesticide contamination. They do not spend much time talking about that at the Whole Foods store.

The most delicious irony is this: the parts of farming that are the most "industrial" are the most likely to be owned by the kind of family farmers that elicit such a positive response from the consumer. Corn farms are almost all owned and managed by small family farmers. But corn farmers salivate at the thought of one more biotech breakthrough, use vast amounts of energy to increase production, and raise large quantities of an indistinguishable commodity to sell to huge corporations that turn that corn into thousands of industrial products.

Most livestock is produced by family farms, and even the poultry industry, with its contracts and vertical integration, relies on family farms to contract for the production of the birds. Despite the obvious change in scale over time, family farms, like ours, still meet around the kitchen table, send their kids to the same small schools, sit in the same church pew, and belong to the same civic organizations our parents and grandparents did. We may be industrial by some definition, but not our own. Reality is messier than it appears in the book my tormentor was reading, and farming more complicated than a simple morality play.

On the desk in front of me are a dozen books, all hugely critical of present-day farming. Farmers are often given a pass in these books, painted as either naïve tools of corporate greed, or economic nullities forced into their present circumstances by the unrelenting forces of the twin grindstones of corporate greed and unfeeling markets. To the farmer on the ground, though, a farmer blessed with free choice and hard won experience, the moral choices aren't quite so easy. Biotech crops actually cut the use of chemicals, and increase food safety. Are people who refuse to use them my moral superiors? Herbicides cut the need for tillage, which decreases soil erosion by millions of tons. The biggest environmental harm I have done as a farmer is the topsoil (and nutrients) I used to send down the Missouri River to the Gulf of Mexico before we began to practice no-till farming, made possible only by the use of herbicides. The combination of herbicides and genetically modified seed has made my farm more sustainable, not less, and actually reduces the pollution I send down the river.

Finally, consumers benefit from cheap food. If you think they don't, just remember the headlines after food prices began increasing in 2007 and 2008, including the study by the Food and Agriculture Organization of the United Nations announcing that 50 million additional people are now hungry because of increasing food prices. Only "industrial farming" can possibly meet the demands of an increasing population and increased demand for food as a result of growing incomes.

So the stakes in this argument are even higher. Farmers can raise food in different ways if that is what the market wants. It is important, though, that even people riding in airplanes know that there are environmental and food safety costs to whatever kind of farming we choose.

Pigs in a Pen

In his book *Dominion*, author Mathew Scully calls "factory farming" an "obvious moral evil so sickening and horrendous it would leave us ashen." Scully, a speechwriter for the second President Bush, can hardly be called a man of the left. Just to make sure the point is not lost, he quotes the conservative historian Paul Johnson a page later:

> The rise of factory farming, whereby food producers cannot remain competitive except by subjecting animals to unspeakable deprivation, has hastened this process. The human spirit revolts at what we have been doing.

Arizona and Florida have outlawed pig gestation crates, and California recently passed, overwhelmingly, a ballot initiative doing the same. There is no doubt that Scully and Johnson have the wind at their backs, and confinement raising of livestock may well be outlawed everywhere. And only a person so callous as to have a spirit that cannot be revolted, or so hardened to any kind of morality that he could countenance an obvious moral evil, could say a word in defense of caging animals during their production. In the quote above, Paul Johnson is forecasting a move toward vegetarianism. But if we assume, at least for the present, that most of us will continue to eat meat, let me dive in where most fear to tread.

Protected from the weather and predators, today's turkeys may not be aware that they are a part of a morally reprehensible system.

Lynn Niemann was a neighbor of my family's, a farmer with a vision. He began raising turkeys on a field near his house around 1956. They were, I suppose, what we would now call "free range" turkeys. Turkeys raised in a natural manner, with no roof over their heads, just gamboling around in the pasture, as God surely intended. Free to eat grasshoppers, and grass, and scratch for grubs and worms. And also free to serve as prey for weasels, who kill turkeys by slitting their necks and practicing exsanguination. Weasels were a problem, but not as much a threat as one of our typically violent early summer thunderstorms. It seems that turkeys, at least young ones, are not smart enough to come in out of the rain, and will stand outside in a downpour, with beaks open and eyes skyward, until they drown. One night Niemann lost 4,000 turkeys to drowning, along with his dream, and his farm.

Now, turkeys are raised in large open sheds. Chickens and turkeys raised for meat are not grown in cages. As the critics of "industrial farming" like to point out, the sheds get quite crowded by the time Thanksgiving rolls around and the turkeys are fully grown. And yes, the birds are bedded in sawdust, so the turkeys do walk around in their own waste. Although the turkeys don't seem to mind, this quite clearly disgusts the various authors I've read whom have actually visited a turkey farm. But none of those authors, whose descriptions of the horrors of modern poultry production have a certain sameness, were there when Neimann picked up those 4,000 dead turkeys. Sheds are expensive, and it was easier to raise turkeys in open, inexpensive pastures. But that type of production really was hard on the turkeys. Protected from the weather and predators, today's turkeys may not be aware that they are a part of a morally reprehensible system.

We are clearly in the process of deciding that we will not continue to raise animals the way we do now.

Like most young people in my part of the world, I was a 4-H member. Raising cattle and hogs, showing them at the county fair, and then sending to slaughter those animals that we had spent the summer feeding, washing, and training. We would then tour the packing house, where our friend was hung on a rail, with his loin eye measured and his carcass evaluated. We farm kids got an early start on dulling our moral sensibilities. I'm still proud of my win in the Atchison County Carcass competition of 1969, as it is the only trophy I have ever received. We raised the hogs in a shed, or farrowing (birthing) house. On one side were eight crates of the kind that the good citizens of California have outlawed. On the other were the kind of wooden pens that our critics would have us use, where the sow could turn around, lie down, and presumably act in a natural way. Which included lying down on my 4-H project, killing several piglets, and forcing me to clean up the mess when I did my chores before school. The crates protect the piglets from their mothers. Farmers do not cage their hogs because of sadism, but because dead pigs are a drag on the profit margin, and because being crushed by your mother really is an awful way to go. As is being eaten by your mother, which I've seen sows do to newborn pigs as well.

I warned you that farming is still dirty and bloody, and I wasn't kidding. So let's talk about manure. It is an article of faith amongst the agri-intellectuals that we no longer use manure as fertilizer. To quote Dr. Michael Fox in his book *Eating with a Conscience*, "The animal waste is not going back to the land from which the animal feed originated." Or Bill McKibben, in his book *Deep Economy*, writing about modern livestock production: "But this concentrates the waste in one place, where instead of being useful fertilizer to spread on crop fields it becomes a toxic threat."

In my inbox is an email from our farm's neighbor, who raises thousands of hogs in close proximity to our farm, and several of my family member's houses as well. The email outlines the amount and chemical analysis of the manure that will be spread on our fields this fall, manure that will replace dozens of tons of commercial fertilizer. The manure is captured underneath the hog houses in cement pits, and is knifed into the soil after the crops are harvested. At no time is it exposed to erosion, and it is an extremely valuable resource, one which farmers use to its fullest extent, just as they have since agriculture began.

In the southern part of Missouri, there is an extensive poultry industry in areas of the state where the soil is poor. The farmers there spread the poultry litter on pasture, and the advent of poultry barns made cattle production possible in areas that used to be waste ground. The "industrial" poultry houses are owned by family farmers, who have then used the byproducts to produce beef in areas where cattle couldn't survive before. McKibben is certain that the contracts these farmers sign with companies like Tyson are unfair, and the farmers might agree. But they like those cows, so there is a waiting list for new chicken barns. In some areas, there is indeed more manure than available cropland. But the trend in the industry, thankfully, is toward a dispersion of animals and manure, as the value of the manure increases, and the cost of transporting the manure becomes prohibitive.

We Can't Change Nature

The largest producer of pigs in the United States has promised to gradually end the use of hog crates. The Humane Society promises to take their initiative drive to outlaw farrowing crates and poultry cages to more states. Many of the counties in my own state of Missouri have chosen to outlaw the building of confinement facilities. Barack Obama has been harshly critical of animal agriculture. We are clearly in the process of deciding that we will not continue to raise animals the way we do now. Because other countries may not share our sensibilities, we'll have to withdraw or amend free trade agreements to keep any semblance of a livestock industry.

We can do that, and we may be a better society for it, but we can't change nature. Pigs will be allowed to "return to their mire," as Kipling had it, but they'll also be crushed and eaten by their mothers. Chickens will provide lunch to any number of predators, and some number of chickens will die as flocks establish their pecking order.

I use all the animal manure available to me, and do everything I can to reduce the amount of commercial fertilizers I use. . . . But none of those things will completely replace commercial fertilizer.

In recent years, the cost of producing pork dropped as farmers increased feed efficiency (the amount of feed needed to produce a pound of pork) by 20 percent. Free-range chickens and pigs will increase the price of food, using more energy and water to produce the extra grain required for the same amount of meat, and some people will go hungry. It is also instructive that the first company to move away from farrowing crates is the largest producer of pigs. Changing the way we raise animals will not necessarily change the scale of the companies involved in the industry. If we are about to require more expensive ways of producing food, the largest and most well-capitalized farms will have the least trouble adapting.

The Omnivores' Delusions

Michael Pollan, in an 8,000-word essay in the New York Times Magazine, took the expected swipes at animal agriculture. But his truly radical prescriptions had to do with raising of crops. Pollan, who seemed to be aware of the nitrogen problem in his book *The Omnivore's Dilemma*, left nuance behind, as well as the laws of chemistry, in his recommendations. The nitrogen problem is this: without nitrogen, we do not have life. Until we learned to produce nitrogen from natural gas early in the last century, the only way to get nitrogen was through nitrogen produced by plants called legumes, or from small amounts of nitrogen that are produced by lightning strikes. The amount of life the earth could support was limited by the amount of nitrogen available for crop production.

In his book, Pollan quotes geographer Vaclav Smil to the effect that 40 percent of the people alive today would not be alive without the ability to artificially synthesize nitrogen. But in his directive on food policy, Pollan damns agriculture's dependence on fossil fuels, and urges the president to encourage agriculture to move away from expensive and declining supplies of natural gas toward the unlimited sunshine that supported life, and agriculture, as recently as the 1940s. Now, why didn't I think of that?

Well, I did. I've raised clover and alfalfa for the nitrogen they produce, and half the time my land is planted to soybeans, another nitrogen producing legume. Pollan writes as if all of his ideas are new, but my father tells of agriculture extension meetings in the late 1950s entitled "Clover and Corn, the Road to Profitability." Farmers know that organic farming was the default position of agriculture for thousands of years, years when hunger was just around the corner for even advanced societies. I use all the animal manure available to me, and do everything I can to reduce the amount of commercial fertilizers I use. When corn genetically modified to use nitrogen more efficiently enters the market, as it soon will, I will use it as well. But none of those things will completely replace commercial fertilizer.

Norman Borlaug, founder of the green revolution, estimates that the amount of nitrogen available naturally would only support a worldwide population of 4 billion souls or so. He further remarks that we would need another 5 billion cows to produce enough manure to fertilize our present crops with "natural" fertilizer. That would play havoc with global warming. And cows do not produce nitrogen from the air, but only from the forages they eat, so to produce more manure we will have to plant more forages. Most of the critics of industrial farming maintain the contradictory positions that we should increase the use of manure as a fertilizer, and decrease our consumption of meat. Pollan would solve the problem with cover crops, planted after the corn crop is harvested, and with mandatory composting. Pollan should talk to some actual farmers before he presumes to advise a president.

> *We are producing twice the food we did in 1960 on less land, and commercial nitrogen is one of the main reasons why.*

Pollan tells of flying over the upper Midwest in the winter, and seeing the black, fallow soil. I suppose one sees what one wants to see, but we have not had the kind of tillage implement on our farm that would produce black soil in nearly 20 years. Pollan would provide our nitrogen by planting those black fields to nitrogen-producing cover crops after the cash crops are harvested. This is a fine plan, one that farmers have known about for generations. And sometimes it would even work. But not last year, as we finished harvest in November in a freezing rain. It is hard to think of a legume that would have done its thing between then and corn planting time. Plants do not grow very well in freezing weather, a fact that would evidently surprise Pollan.

And even if we could have gotten a legume established last fall, it would not have fixed any nitrogen before planting time. We used to plant corn in late May, plowing down our green manure and killing the first flush of weeds. But that meant the corn would enter its crucial growing period during the hottest, driest parts of the summer, and that soil erosion would be increased because the land was bare during drenching spring rains. Now we plant in early April, best utilizing our spring rains, and ensuring that pollination occurs before the dog days of August.

A few other problems come to mind. The last time I planted a cover crop, the clover provided a perfect habitat in early spring for bugs, bugs that I had to kill with an insecticide. We do not normally apply insecticides, but we did that year. Of course, you can provide nitrogen with legumes by using a longer crop rotation, growing clover one year and corn the next. But that uses twice as much water to produce a corn crop, and takes twice as much land to produce the same number of bushels. We are producing twice the food we did in 1960 on less land, and commercial nitrogen is one of the main reasons why. It may be that we decide we would rather spend land and water than energy, but Pollan never mentions that we are faced with that choice.

His other grand idea is mandatory household composting, with the compost delivered to farmers free of charge. Why not? Compost is a valuable soil amendment, and if somebody else is paying to deliver it to my farm, then bring it on. But it will not do much to solve the nitrogen problem. Household compost has somewhere between 1 and 5 percent nitrogen, and not all that nitrogen is available to crops the first year. Presently, we are applying about 150 pounds of nitrogen per acre to corn, and crediting about 40 pounds per acre from the preceding years soybean crop. Let's assume a 5 percent nitrogen rate, or about 100 pounds of nitrogen per ton of compost. That would require 3,000 pounds of compost per acre. Or about 150,000 tons for the corn raised in our county. The average truck carries about 20 tons. Picture 7,500 trucks traveling from New York City to our small county here in the Midwest, delivering compost. Five million truckloads to fertilize the country's corn crop. Now, that would be a carbon footprint!

Pollan thinks farmers use commercial fertilizer because it is easier, and because it is cheap. Pollan is right. But those are perfectly defensible reasons. Nitrogen quadrupled in price over the last several years, and farmers are still using it, albeit more cautiously. We are using GPS monitors on all of our equipment to ensure that we do not use too much, and our production of corn per pound of nitrogen is rapidly increasing. On our farm, we have increased yields about 50 percent during my career, while applying about the same amount of nitrogen we did when I began farming. That fortunate trend will increase even faster with the advent of new GMO hybrids. But as much as Pollan might desire it, even President Obama cannot reshuffle the chemical deck that nature has dealt. Energy may well get much more expensive, and peak oil production may have been reached. But food production will have a claim on fossil fuels long after we have learned how to use renewables and nuclear power to handle many of our other energy needs.

Farming and Connectedness

Much of farming is more "industrial," more technical, and more complex than it used to be. Farmers farm more acres, and are less close to the ground and their animals than they were in the past. Almost all critics of industrial agriculture bemoan this loss of closeness, this "connectedness," to use author Rod Dreher's term. It is a given in most of the writing about agriculture that the knowledge and experience of the organic farmer is what makes him so unique and so important. The "industrial farmer," on the other hand, is a mere pawn of Cargill, backed into his ignorant way of life by forces too large, too far from the farm, and too powerful to resist. Concern about this alienation, both between farmers and the land, and between consumers and their food supply, is what drives much of the literature about agriculture.

The distance between the farmer and what he grows has certainly increased, but, believe me, if we weren't closely connected, we wouldn't still be farming. It's important to our critics that they emphasize this alienation, because they have to ignore the "industrial" farmer's experience and knowledge to say the things they do about farming.

But farmers have reasons for their actions, and society should listen to them as we embark upon this reappraisal of our agricultural system. I use chemicals and diesel fuel to accomplish the tasks my grandfather used to do with sweat, and I use a computer instead of a lined notebook and a pencil, but I'm still farming the same land he did 80 years ago, and the fund of knowledge that our family has accumulated about our small part of Missouri is valuable. And everything I know and I have learned tells me this: we have to farm "industrially" to feed the world, and by using those "industrial" tools sensibly, we can accomplish that task and leave my grandchildren a prosperous and productive farm, while protecting the land, water, and air around us.

Killing the Chicken

Tom Pittman

Tom Pittman has a PhD in information science from the University of California at Santa Cruz.

Whenever somebody claims "This (activity) is more spiritual than that one," I need to give due diligence to determine whether I should adjust my own spiritual life to encompass the claimed benefit, or if the claim is really nothing more than "I like my secular tradition more than your secular tradition." After substantial research, I think your chicken farm article falls into the latter category.

I do not begrudge author Bret Mavrich any spiritual benefit he might get from using small tools to kill a chicken in his hand, and he should not deny my spiritual benefit from using larger tools to kill many chickens a thousand miles away: we both thank God for providing chickens for us to eat, and for farmers to grow them, whether that be in small farms like Lamppost as featured in his article, or in factory farms like Tyson runs elsewhere in the country.

Make no mistake, Christians around the world have derived substantial spiritual (as well as financial) benefit from factory farms and processed food, because those scorned links in the food chain have freed up millions of people from the drudge of growing and preparing their own food, so that they can do other things to create wealth in this country, making it the richest country in the world and in all time. Most people squander their share of that wealth and freedom in "riotous living" but many have invested a portion of it to pay for a smaller number of the same people (also not needed to grow food) to preach the gospel in countries where the population is still largely preoccupied in growing and processing their own food in the manner recommended by Mavrich and/or the owners of Lamppost, and who therefore cannot afford to pay their own pastors and missionaries. Other people freed from food preparation used their time to invent computers and to program them to do publishing kinds of things, so that Christianity Today can tell us about Lamppost farm and C.S. Lewis and other spiritually uplifting things, which would not be possible if this were not the wealthiest country in the world, largely because we uniquely do not need to spend vast amounts of time in farming and food preparation and clothing manufacture and other activities that so filled the days of our great grandparents.

Multiply that times the entire country, and you have a huge amount of labor that can be invested in all kinds of other stuff (besides food preparation), which creates wealth exponentially, with enough left over for us to be God's benefactors to the world.

Factory farms and processed food did that for us, but it's not obvious. Lamppost farm has a website with an email address, and the owners, Steve & Melanie Montgomery were kind enough to answer my questions. I also searched the internet for differences between organic and factory farming methods. The food value appears to be scientifically indistinguishable, and after you demythologize the hype there aren't a lot of other big differences, except labor. Everybody agrees that organic farming is labor intensive, but hardly anybody will say how much, probably because it looks so bad. I found one farmer who admitted that his organic farm used three times as much labor as the same acreage would by conventional farming methods. Another wanted cooks everywhere to be raising and killing (and presumably plucking by hand) their own chickens.

I buy TV dinners or canned soup for about $1 each, slightly more now after the Obama tax on poor people (aka inflation) is added, and I heat them in five minutes in a microwave, during which time I can do other things. I can prepare a comparable meal from fresh ingredients in an hour or two of total attention—assuming I do not restrict my purchases to local produce, which there isn't any here this time of year. If I search out and buy local when it is available, then preserve it for the winter, it doubles or triples the time I would spend on feeding myself from California and Arizona produce. That means I'd spend essentially all day just on food preparation. As a computer programmer, I can earn 500 times the cost of that TV dinner or can of soup in the time it takes me to prepare it from local fresh. That doesn't seem like a good investment of the "talent" God entrusted to me. If I eat TV dinners and cheap soup and spend my time programming Bible translation software (which I do), then I can work a very long time on the money I earned programming computers for pay 20 years ago, when I ate better but still spent my time more productively than growing and preparing food. I tried growing my own garden, but gave it up when it consumed a couple hours a day picking big worms off tomatoes I can otherwise buy all year around for $1/week. It's not a good use of my time. Different people will of course have different multipliers. If God had made me a plumber or a truck driver or a school teacher, I might earn a little less per hour than I can as a programmer, but still far more than the cost of buying factory food instead of making it myself in the same time I would otherwise be working.

Multiply that times the entire country, and you have a huge amount of labor that can be invested in all kinds of other stuff (besides food preparation), which creates wealth exponentially, with enough left over for us to be God's benefactors to the world, in food and technology as well as Christianity. We can even afford to let some people grow organic food (at a high price) and occasionally prepare things from scratch, if that makes them feel good about thanking God for it. I have done some recreational cooking myself—but not very often: it's not a good use of my time.

I have also spent too much time writing this letter. I need to get back to the work God gave me to do—and to thanking God for produce farms in California and truckers who drive it 2000 miles to the local grocery stores, and for factory farms in Iowa and Arkansas that package up processed foods that I can eat so inexpensively, and for putting lots of oil in the ground in Saudi Arabia so it doesn't cost much to get that factory food from the farms and food processors to my grocery store and then to my house. And I can also thank God that there are so many people with time (and money, because they don't have to spend all day in food preparation) who are willing to study God's Word and to preach the gospel here and elsewhere. God is awesome!

Factory Farming Helps Feed People Around the World

Maureen Ogle

Maureen Ogle is an historian and the author of In Meat We Trust.

Decided I'd better come out of hiding for this one.[1]

Muckraking Journalism

The current issue of *Rolling Stone* magazine features a long story about animal rights activists working undercover at livestock confinement operations. It's a classic, high-quality example of muckraking journalism. That, I hasten to add, is not a criticism. The piece should be taken for what it is: an effort to persuade readers to embrace a specific position on a contentious issue.

The story, written by Paul Solotaroff, employs the usual tactics of muckraking story-making: loaded language, vague claims, twisted facts, and leaps of illogic. Again, this isn't criticism. There's a place for this kind of literature in our society and as I noted above, this is a fine example.[2]

I'm not interested in refuting the story's contents. Nor am I interested in defending the "other side."[3]

Rather, my interest, as a historian and a citizen, is in the essay's function. Solotaroff's story serves as an incendiary device in an ongoing, and important, cultural war: the battle over America's agrarian future. The debate about factory-like livestock production is less about specific evils than it is about the future of agriculture in American society and culture; about agriculture's role in our national identity.

Agrarian Mythology

As many Americans know, the agrarian past looms large in both our national identity and mythology: The nation was founded by the sturdy yeoman, the rugged individual, etc. Those who work the land are the best among us, etc. Rural values are the bedrock of American society; threaten those and the republic itself is threatened, etc. (See, for example, [novelist, activist, and farmer] Wendell Berry.)

This mythology is just that: mythology. Historically, first in the colonies and then in the new United States, American farmers were less interested in yeoman "independence" than in earning profits from a national and global market for food stuffs. (And make no mistake: American agriculture has served a global market since the 1600s.)

These days, only a few hundred thousand Americans work as "farmers." But this powerful agrarian mythology endures. It remains part of who we Americans imagine ourselves to be.[4]

As we debate our agrarian future, we must weigh that future against the needs of people around the world (about whom most of us claim we care).

Indeed, the critique of livestock production and "factory" farming is based on that myth. Ask a critic about the failings of current farming methods and she'll say something along the lines of "We'd be better off if we could return to the way things used to be. When farms were small and owned by families who relied on nature rather than chemicals and who grazed livestock on pasture instead of imprisoning them in confinement."

When critics imagine the future of American agriculture, they envision a return to (an imagined) past because that imagined past is central to what it means to be an American.

But that future isn't only about "us." For better or for worse, our modern livestock production system was designed to supply meat protein to the rest of the world. As we debate our agrarian future, we must weigh that future against the needs of people around the world (about whom most of us claim we care). A big decision, right?

Which is why *Rolling Stone*'s article fails the magazine's readers; fails the citizenry it was presumably written to serve. If we're going to have a serious, substantive discussion about agriculture's future, we need more facts and less loaded, emotionally skewed coverage.

By all means: read the story in *Rolling Stone*. Just take it for what it is: an incendiary device rather than a substantive contribution to an important discussion.

Notes

1. And I am in hiding of sorts. Here's a fact: having spent seven years ensconced in my brain writing a book, now that said book is finished the only place I want to be is in the 3-dimensional world. Translation: at the moment, I have little interest in writing, even something as short, easy as a blog entry. What can I say? I'm human.

2. Essays like this exist to do one thing: rally the troops. And, in this case, raise money for organizations devoted to whatever cause is at stake. In this case, it's a safe bet that the Humane Society of the United States, which is featured in the report, will enjoy an uptick in contributions.

3. I'll just say this: Solotaroff's piece rests in large part on a grossly inaccurate telling of how and why factory farms came to be in this country; on the who/what/when/why behind factory farms. That's understandable: he's not a

historian and can't be expected to know that history. But he's also not interested in accuracy because it works against his larger goal of rallying the troops.

4. As to that agrarian mythology. How "real," I wonder, is that part of the American past to most Americans today? For immigrants from, say, Sudan or Bosnia or China or Mexico, surely that aspect of the "meaning" of America is irrelevant. Which makes the yearning to return to that imagined past even more impractical—and, yes, irrelevant. All the more reason, then, for critics of contemporary agriculture to exercise more care with the solutions they propose to the problems they perceive.

CHAPTER 3

Current
CONTROVERSIES

Does Hunting Violate Animal Rights?

Chapter Preface

Wolves, which were especially hated because of their propensity to eat livestock, were essentially hunted to extinction in the United States in the early twentieth century. They were put on the endangered species list in 1974, making it illegal to hunt them—though it didn't much matter, since there were hardly any to hunt by that time. In 1995, however, the US Fish and Wildlife Service reintroduced wolves from Canada to Yellowstone National Park, and by 2005 the population had rebounded to approximately two thousand animals. This kicked off a heated debate: should people be allowed to hunt wolves again? Both federal and state authorities have gone back and forth on when, where, and how it should be legitimate to hunt wolves.

Ron Meador, writing at the website Minnpost, argues that some wolf hunting is necessary. Meador paraphrased wolf expert David Mech, saying:

> I am concerned with the survival of wolves as a species, and that means I can't be concerned about saving every individual wolf. If we put wolves on a pedestal above all other species that we hunt, people will take the law into their hands, and before long we'll be right back to the time when, for most folks, the only good wolf was a dead wolf. Sooner or later we're going to have to have a hunt.[1]

Meador argues that the hunting should be carefully regulated. He points out that livestock farmers are allowed to shoot wolves on their property, and that it's difficult to know what that will do to the wolf population. Given that wolf were

---

1. Ron Meador, "Minnesota's Wolf Harvest Takes Shape with Reliance on Trapping and Baiting," Minnpost, September 18, 2012. http://www.minnpost.com/earth-journal /2012/09/minnesotas-wolf-harvest-takes-shape-reliance-trapping-and-baiting.

so recently endangered, he argues that hunting should only be reinstituted with great caution.

The *Missoulian* makes a similar argument in reference to Montana's wolf population. The editorial points out that the wolf population in Montana is growing, and that the efforts to limit it through hunting have not been as successful as the state hoped, since hunters did not kill as many wolves in the 2012 season as expected. However, the *Missoulan* argues, the answer is not to resort to trapping, which is cruel and painful and which might end up trapping other animals. "Let's not increase the likelihood of injuring 'non-target' species—or even start down that road,"[2] the newspaper says in an editorial. Instead, the newspaper suggests that the wolf-kill limit for hunters be expanded.

The rest of this chapter looks at other issues surrounding animal hunting and animal welfare, such as the ethics of culling deer and the relationship between hunting and conservation.

---

2. *Missoulian*, "Wolf Trapping Is Cruel and Unnecessary," July 11, 2012. http://missoulian.com/news/opinion/editorial/wolf-trapping-is-cruel-and-unnecessary/article_febd699c-cb61-11e1-9e72-0019bb2963f4.html.

Hunting Is Cruel and Unnecessary

In Defense of Animals

In Defense of Animals is an international animal rights and rescue organization dedicated to protecting the rights, welfare, and habitats of animals.

Hunting may have played an important role, next to plant gathering and scavenging, for human survival in prehistoric times, but the modern "sportsman" stalks and kills animals for "recreation." Hunting is a violent and cowardly form of outdoor "entertainment" that kills hundreds of millions of animals every year, many of whom are wounded and die a slow and painful death.

Hunters cause injuries, pain and suffering to defenseless animals, destroy their families and habitat, and leave terrified and dependent baby animals behind to starve to death. Because state wildlife agencies are primarily funded by hunting, trapping and fishing licenses, today's wildlife management actively promotes the killing of wild animals, and joined by a powerful hunting lobby even sells wildlife trophy hunts to those who enjoy killing them. For instance, the California Department of Fish and Wildlife (CDFW) just received $45,000 from the sale of a killing tag for California Desert Bighorn Sheep, which was sold at the 41st Safari Club International Convention in Reno, Nevada. Getting the trophy is an unwritten guarantee.

Pain and Suffering

A mere six percent of the human U.S. population hunts—compared to the nearly 71.8 million people who enjoyed watching wildlife in 2011. Hunting is permitted on 60 percent of U.S. public lands, including in over 50 percent of wildlife refuges, many national forests and state parks; on federal land alone (more than half a billion acres), more than 200 million animals are killed every year.

Quick kills are rare, and many animals suffer prolonged, painful deaths when hunters severely injure but fail to kill them. Bow hunting exacerbates the problem, evidenced by dozens of scientific studies that have shown that bow hunting yields more than a 50 percent wounding and crippling rate. Some hunting groups promote shooting animals in the face or in the gut, which is a horrifically painful way to die.

Several states (AZ, ID, MT, OR, UT, WY) allow a spring bear hunt during the months when bears emerge from hibernation. These bears are not only still lethargic, which makes them easy targets for hunters, but many of the females are either pregnant or lactating. Mother bears are often shot while out and about foraging, while hiding their cubs in trees or leaving them in their dens. When mother bears are killed, their nursing cubs have little to no chance of survival as they will either starve or be killed by predators.

Wildlife management, population control and wildlife conservation are euphemisms for killing—hunting, trapping and fishing for fun.

The stress that hunting inflicts on animals—the noise, the fear, and the constant chase—severely restricts their ability to eat adequately and store the fat and energy they need to survive the winter. Hunting also disrupts migration and hibernation, and the campfires, recreational vehicles and trash adversely affect both wildlife and the environment. For animals like wolves, who mate for life and have close-knit family units, hunting can destroy entire communities.

Hunting Is Not Sport

Hunting is often called a "sport," to disguise a cruel, needless killing spree as a socially acceptable activity. However, the concept of sport involves competition between two consenting parties, adherence to rules and fairness ensured by an intervening referee, and achieving highest scores but not death as the goal of the sporting events. In hunting, the animal is forced to "participate" in a live-or-die situation that always leads to the death of the animal, whereas the hunter leaves, his/her life never remotely at stake.

Despite hunters' common claim of adhering to a "fair chase" code, there is no such thing. With an arsenal of rifles, shotguns, muzzleloaders, handguns, bows and arrows, hunters kill more than 200 million animals yearly—likely crippling, orphaning, and harassing millions more. The annual death toll in the U.S. includes 42 million mourning doves, 30 million squirrels, 28 million quail, 25 million rabbits, 20 million pheasants, 14 million ducks, 6 million deer, and thousands of geese, bears, moose, elk, antelope, swans, cougars, turkeys, wolves, foxes, coyotes, bobcats, boars, and other woodland creatures. Hunters also frequently use food and electronic callers to lure unsuspecting animals in front of their weapons. The truth is, the animal, no matter how well-adapted to escaping natural predators she or he may be, has virtually no way to escape death once he or she is in the cross hairs of a scope mounted on a rifle or a cross bow.

Wildlife management, population control and wildlife conservation are euphemisms for killing—hunting, trapping and fishing for fun. A percentage of the wild animal population is specifically mandated to be killed. Hunters want us to believe that killing animals equals population control equals conservation, when in fact hunting causes overpopulation of deer, the hunters' preferred victim species, destroys animal families, and leads to ecological disruption as well as skewed population dynamics. Because state wildlife agencies are primarily funded by hunters and other wildlife killers, programs are in place to manipulate habitat and artificially bolster "game" populations while ignoring "non-game" species. These programs lead to overpopulation and unbalanced ecosystems by favoring "buck only" hunts, pen-raising pheasants and other birds as living targets for hunters, transporting wild turkeys, raccoons and other species across state's lines to boost populations for hunters and trappers to kill, and by exterminating predators such as wolves and mountain lions, in order to increase "prey" animals like elk and deer to then justify hunting as needed for "population control."

While hunters and so-called wildlife professionals pretend to have control over ecosystems and the animals they kill, natural predators such as wolves, mountain lions and bears are the real ecosystem managers.

Hunting Contributes to Species Extinction

Hunting has contributed to the historical extinction of animal species all over the world, including the Southern Appalachian birds, the passenger pigeon and the Carolina parakeet (the only member of the parrot family native to the eastern United States), the eastern elk, the eastern cougar, the Tasmanian tiger and the great auk.

Wildlife managers and hunters treat wild animals like a crop, of which a percentage can be "harvested" annually—to them, wild animals are no different than a field of wheat. This "selective" science, with its exclusive focus on numbers to be killed, ignores the science that shows that nonhumans, just like humans, have the same capabilities to experience emotions, and that they have families and other social associations built on multi-leveled relationships.

While hunters and so-called wildlife professionals pretend to have control over ecosystems and the animals they kill, natural predators such as wolves, mountain lions and bears are the real ecosystem managers, if allowed to survive naturally. For instance, the reintroduction of wolves to Yellowstone National Park (YNP) caused "ripple effects" throughout the ecosystem, with an increase in 'biodiversity,' including a higher occurrence of beavers, several bird and plant species, and natural habitat and stream recovery.

What You Can Do

Join In Defense of Animals (IDA) and support our efforts to end recreational hunting. Before you support a "wildlife" or "conservation" group, ask about its position on hunting and trapping. Some groups, including the National Wildlife Federation, Defenders of Wildlife, the National Audubon Society, the Izaak Walton League, the Wilderness Society, and the World Wildlife Fund support recreational hunting or they do not oppose it.

If you are a student of environmental studies, conservation and natural resource management or wildlife biology, challenge the concept of hunting as the foundation for wildlife conservation/management. Become familiar with nonlethal human/wildlife conflict solutions, and educate your classmates, your professors and your community. Attend public meetings of your state's wildlife agency, voice your opinion against hunting in their public commenting process. Speak up, write letters and comments, and encourage others to do the same.

Join or form an anti-hunting organization and help with spreading the word about the injustice done against wild animals by hunters and state wildlife agencies. Contact your state's Governor and wildlife agency, and request equal consideration of non-hunters in employment opportunities, and equal representation of non-hunters in any decision-making process about wildlife.

Canned Hunting of Lions Is Cruel and Inhumane

Jerome Flynn

Jerome Flynn is a British actor and singer.

The survival of white lions [as] a free roaming species is hanging by a thread. There is an abominable, growing, legal industry that threatens all the lions of South Africa, both tawny and white, a practice that is so despicable it makes one's stomach shudder at how disconnected from his heart man can be.

It is known as "canned hunting." This practice involves taking cubs from their captive mothers at birth. That means the mothers can go into oestrus and breed again within a few months, rather than every 2 or 3 years as they would in the wild.

The cubs will then be used in the 'cub-petting' industry aimed at unsuspecting tourists and celebrities. Then, when they grow too big to be cuddled, if they are very lucky, they end up in a zoo, but most likely they will be drugged and then gunned down in captivity by a wealthy foreigner, paying up to £50,000 for the right to do so.

These helpless young lions, by now are not even a shadow of their natural selves, with no fear of humans and nowhere to escape to even if they wanted to. There is no hunting involved here; it is just cold blooded slaughter of a tame animal.

An animal, that since human culture began, has been revered as the King of all animals. A beautiful, supremely majestic creature whose name, nature and image we have used through the millennia as symbols of strength, divinity, courage and grace.

The Lion is surely mankind's ultimate power animal, and yet here we are in the 21st century, with a legal industry that strips away all their power, respect and freedom, wrecking their genetics through interbreeding so that reintroduction into the wild becomes impossible, and then gunning them down for the sake of what?

Man's twisted ego that somehow believes he can claim that power for himself. Its head may end up as a trophy on a wall, and very likely its bones will find their way into another expanding Chinese industry that sells lion bone as a tonic to boost our sex drive. How low have we fallen?

There are now over twice as many captive lions in South Africa as there are running wild and these shameful industries mean that poaching of the free lions is increasing.

We should roar our support for these beautiful regal cousins, who have given us so much.

Recent environmental studies have put lions firmly on the endangered list. However, the rare White Lions, known as the sacred animal of Africa, are even more prized as trophies, so those few of them that are free are acutely endangered, to say the least.

If this is a cause that tugs at your heart, as it has mine, there's something coming along soon that we can all show up for, to help our lion friends, and in so doing help ourselves.

On 15 March [2014], there is a Global March for Lions taking place in over 55 cities across the world, to put pressure on the South African president to ban canned and trophy hunting for good, to demand that our governments ban the importation of all lion parts and trophies (why on Earth would this be legal)? and to demand that China ban all products containing lion bone.

I've been to visit these white lions for myself. Words just don't get close when trying to sum up what it is to sit in their majestic presence. We should roar our support for these beautiful regal cousins, who have given us so much, especially here in the UK. From Richard the Lionheart to the British Lions, these Great Cats are etched deep into our nation's psyche.

Now it is our turn to be lionhearted, to stand up for them and demand that the King of animals live the life of majesty and freedom that nature intended.

Faroe Islands Whale Hunting Is Cruel and Dangerous

Gavin Haines

Gavin Haines is a freelance journalist and photographer specializing in environmental and travel reporting.

Under a brooding sky on the Faroe Islands, I'm engaged in a mental battle. I'm forming, adjusting and reforming opinion on a controversial practice that has been taking place here for centuries; the pilot whale hunt.

The Hunt

Elsewhere on the islands, another battle is taking place. Fishermen are chasing down a pod of pilot whales, fighting tides and inclement weather as they manoeuvre their boats to drive the mammals into shallow water, where men with knives will wade into the surf to kill them.

The sea will turn red, dorsal fins will splash frantically in the bloody water and dead pilot whales will be dragged ashore. On the beach a quick audit will be conducted before the carcasses are carved up and divided in accordance with ancient rules; the finder (whoever spotted the pod) will get a whole whale, the other hunters will take equal shares and whatever meat is left will be distributed to the local community.

Detach yourself from the ugliness of it and the whale hunt is a shining example of community spirit; when news of a pod sighting spreads, often via Facebook and text message, adults in the vicinity are dismissed from work, children are let out of school and everyone gathers on the beach. There's an almost carnival atmosphere about the occasion.

Locals brave the miserable Faroese weather, as they have done for hundreds of years, waiting for the whales to come. Excitedly, they watch skippers drive the pod inland, before practicing the ancient art of whale sacrifice, which has provided these isolated islands with a food source for generations.

Although food security is no longer an issue here, imported produce is expensive unlike whale meat, which is free. And while islanders enjoy all the modern comforts that we do in Britain, they are much more in touch with the food they eat and its place in the environment; most of the islanders I speak to, think the idea of buying fish from a supermarket is lunacy.

I pitch it to those I meet that the whale hunt is cruel, which is my biggest problem with it. "It's not as bad as people think," says Jóhan Joensen, head chef at Áarstova in Torshavn. "Hunters cut the spine first so it loses all sense of feeling."

Watch videos of the hunt and they tell a different story. Before the fatal wound is delivered, whales are dragged through shallow water by a hook, which hunters drive into their blow holes. Once beached, the fatal blow is delivered (not always on the first attempt) and the mammals writhe around in their own blood as the life ebbs away from them. Locals laugh and smile; you could accuse them of enjoying it too much.

After the first whale is struck, others will be able to taste blood in the water, which must be hugely distressing.

"It is inherently cruel for the whales," says Jennifer Lonsdale, director of the Environmental Investigation Agency. "There is no guarantee the whales will be killed quickly; some will have to wait in turn for their death and others will be driven onto rocks which will cause scratching."

Even if they are killed instantly, Jennifer believes the panic and sense of foreboding beforehand will be extremely stressful for the pilot whales.

"If a mother and child get split up this will cause extreme anxiety," she says. "After the first whale is struck, others will be able to taste blood in the water, which must be hugely distressing. During the hunt you can hear them squeaking, which they don't normally do."

Cruelty and Health

I didn't need Jennifer to tell me it was cruel, I knew that.

But as horrified as I was by the hunt videos I saw, was I really in a position to criticise? What about the fish I've eaten, was their death not distressing? Or the cows, sheep and chickens we breed in Britain for the sole purpose of consuming? Are their lives less important?

"I find it more f***ed up breeding an animal to take to a slaughter house, where men in white coats kill them, put them in plastic packaging and send them to the supermarkets," explains Teitur Lassen, a Faroese singer songwriter. "At least the whales are free in the wild before they are killed."

Salient points from either side, but rather than helping me form opinion on the hunt, they raised questions about my own values. So I talked sustainability with Jennifer, to see if there was anything else that could persuade me to get off the fence.

"The Faroese have conducted research and they speculate there are about three quarters of a million pilot whales in the North Atlantic," she says.

"But what they haven't done is look into how they are split into different populations, which is bad science. It could be that they are eliminating one sub species after another."

However, it is sensible science that provided me with much needed clarity on the subject. Both foreign and Faroese scientists have linked pollutants found in whale meat (which come in the form of organochlorides, mercury and other contaminants), to a cocktail of health problems including cancer, immune deficiencies, male infertility, Parkinson's disease and slower development within children.

"We find it astounding that the government hasn't banned it," says Jennifer. "When we had the BSE problem they banned British beef."

The government haven't completely buried their heads in the sand; they advise men not to consume more than 200g of whale meat per week, while suggesting pregnant women and children abstain.

Possible Ban

Health risks considered the whale hunt seems as pointless as it does cruel. I know it's cultural, I know it's a part of the islands' heritage, but there are Chinese restaurants and pizzerias in the Faroe Islands nowadays, so why chase toxic whales around the ocean?

With more research planned, it has been suggested that, despite the Faroe's fierce protection of its traditions, the whale hunt will eventually be banned on health grounds. Conservationists will hail it as a good day, but it won't be. Instead, it will mark the day when a long, albeit brutal, tradition was swept away not by discourse and changing attitudes, but mankind's degradation of the world's oceans and the life within them.

Canada's Seal Hunt Is Cruel

Lesley Fox

Lesley Fox is the executive director of the Association for the Protection of Fur-Bearing Animals, a nonprofit animal-protection organization based in Burnaby, British Columbia, Canada.

Right now, off the east coast of Canada, the largest marine mammal slaughter in the world is taking place and the images are very disturbing.

It's not my intention to be sensationalist, but it is a fact that when you kill hundreds of thousands of baby seals, the water and ice off the east coast of Canada turns red from all of the blood.

Hundreds of Thousands Dead

Making this year even more shocking than before, the Tories' killing quota is the highest it has ever been—over 468,200 harp, grey and hooded seals are on the chopping block. Literally.

In a world when we marvel in the advances of computer science, medical wonders, and scientific discoveries, there is something seriously wrong with grown men wielding clubs and hooks to bash in the brains of baby seals.

Reports indicate that approximately 95 percent of seals killed are between the ages of two weeks to three months old.

While the killing of the fluffy newborn whitecoat seals is prohibited, once they have begun to molt their pelts (usually around 12 days of age) they are fair game.

Lesley Fox, "Canada's Cruel Seal Hunt Is on Thin Ice This Federal Election," straight .com, April 12, 2011. Copyright © 2011 by Lesley Fox. All rights reserved. Reproduced by permission.

It's easy for sealers to target the babies because these young animals are reluctant to leave the ice, and are not yet strong swimmers.

But despite public outcry and general common sense, the seal slaughter has been going on for decades and with lots of support from the government.

Why is Canada killing seals? That's a good question.

The Department of Fisheries and Oceans says, "As a time-honoured tradition, Canada's seal harvest supports many coastal families who can derive as much as 35% of their annual income from this practice."

But opponents point out that the hunt is cruel and unsustainable, and the sealers, who are essentially commercial fishermen, earn on average less than five percent of their income from killing seals.

Politics

Then there is also the question of political motives.

It's no secret that there is much competition between political parties for votes in the rural areas of Newfoundland, and any party that opposes the seal hunt can consider themselves out of the running.

While no one really knows exactly why Canada loves killing baby seals, a few things are certain. The math doesn't add up.

Furthermore, the primary objective of the Department of Fisheries and Oceans is to ensure there is a booming fishing industry. But fish populations have been dwindling for years and rather than admit to over-fishing or mismanagement playing any part, it is a lot easier for them to just blame the seals for eating all the fish.

Imagine the advantage you would have as a business owner if you could literally kill your main competitor.

While no one really knows exactly why Canada loves killing baby seals, a few things are certain.

The math doesn't add up.

Last year, it was reported that the Canadian seal hunt generated $1.4 million, but taxpayers paid $4.3 million for the Canadian Coast Guard to monitor the area.

And while the government no longer makes direct contributions to the seal hunt, funding is still available for ice breaking vessels and tax breaks seem to be doled out to any sealer who wants one.

It's not only Canadians that are rethinking the seal slaughter; it's entire countries too.

For example, according to the International Fund for Animal Welfare, the government of Newfoundland and Labrador is working to ensure a retroactive tax exemption for sealers who have not been paying the harmonized sales tax on pelts they have sold. Over the past three years alone, this could amount to a $6.3-million "tax break" for the sealing industry.

In addition to all of this funding, the Canadian government continues to subsidize research into developing new markets for seal products and is currently spending your money promoting and marketing seal products overseas.

This is a lot of money to waste on something that the majority of Canadians don't even want.

And it's not only Canadians that are rethinking the seal slaughter; it's entire countries too.

Since 1972, the United States has closed its border to Canada's seal pelts, and just recently the 27-nation European Union followed suit.

Currently, China is our main dumping ground for seal skins, but even that agreement is on thin ice.

Speaking of thin ice, the dwindling market for seal pelts isn't the only problem facing the seal industry. Mother nature is proving to be an obstacle too.

Global warming is melting the ice that the seals rely on to give birth and to nurse their pups. Scientists who work for the Department of Fisheries have recently voiced their concern about the seals' mortality rate, saying it could be far higher than normal because females don't have enough ice to give birth to their pups.

Scientists are also reporting that the ice is breaking up faster than normal, and as a result, many seal pups are drowning because they are too young to survive in the open water.

So considering the global market for seal products is diminishing, and seal populations are in jeopardy because of global warming, the time is right to turn our attention to creating real solutions for the sealers and the animals.

Buy Out the Sealers

Some suggestions include a one-time buyout of the commercial sealing industry where fishermen would be compensated for lost income, and funds could be invested into job retraining or alternative industries.

This isn't a bad idea considering it worked for the whaling industry. In 1972, the Canadian government ended commercial whaling, and licence holders were compensated. Today, the whaling industry has completely reinvented itself with eco-tours and whale watching, which are proving to be a profitable attraction, particularly for tourists.

Whether you are opposed to the inherent cruelty of the seal hunt or the waste of taxpayer money, or it's the impact of global warming on seal populations that concerns you, the time to act is now.

During this election, each one of us has an opportunity to voice our opposition over the seal hunt to our member of

Parliament. Collectively, we have the power to end this slaughter for once and for all—and we can do that at the polls.

Hunting Reconnects Humans with the Natural World

M. Nils Peterson et al.

The following viewpoint was written by M. Nils Peterson, Hans Peter Hansen, Markus J. Peterson, and Tarla Rai Peterson. M. Nils Peterson is associate professor of fisheries, wildlife, and conservation at North Carolina State University. Hans Peter Hansen is an assistant professor of urban and rural development at the Swedish University of Agricultural Science. Markus J. Peterson is a professor of wildlife and fisheries sciences at Texas A&M University. And Tarla Rai Peterson is a visiting professor of environmental communication at the Swedish University of Agricultural Sciences.

The growing alienation between humans and nature may be the most fundamental challenge to sustainability. Human wellbeing depends on improving understanding of the connectedness between humans and natural systems and applying that understanding in the policy arena to meet social challenges. The project of modernity, however, has relied on separating humans from nature, so that humans may control nature. Modern society has masked connections between humans and nature in a variety of ways. Capitalism, one of the most important systems of organizing commodity production in the modern era, relies on alienating workers from the products of their own labor. As "one of the founding principles of capitalist modernism", alienation requires separating sites of production from sites of consumption, thus hiding both the natural and human resources used to construct the face of modernity. As [D.] Harvey notes, "We can take our daily

M. Nils Peterson et al., "How Hunting Strengthens Social Awareness of Coupled Human-Natural Systems," *Wildlife Biology in Practice*, 2010, 6:2, pp. 127–143. Licensed under the Creative Commons Attribution License. Reproduced by permission.

breakfast without a thought for the myriad people who engaged in its production". As the materiality of food becomes more invisible, connections with natural processes, such as life and death, fade.

The isolation between society and nature has accelerated in the last several decades with drivers including urbanization, technology, and commoditization of nature. Urbanization places physical distance between humans and the material sources of their sustenance in nature. Technology provides artificial substitutes for the material and social relationships previously provided by nature. Finally, a late 20th-century wave of privatization and commoditization of everything from land to ideas has rendered the social and material relationships involved in producing food largely invisible.

Social movements including sustainable and just food, alternative trade, worker rights, animal welfare, and 'no child left inside' efforts have attempted to pierce the veil that shrouds production of consumer goods ranging from meat to suburban homes. Despite these efforts, however, modern systems of food production and consumption continue to mask awareness of profound relationships between humans, and natural systems.

Hunting provides an opportunity to link modern humans with natural systems through their food.

In this [viewpoint], we explore how hunting, as a premodern anachronism, may contribute to making society aware of links between human and natural systems by rendering the materiality of food production explicit, and how hunting culture strengthens the symbolic meaning of food in ways that are rooted in natural systems. We begin with a brief summary to contextualize hunting as an anachronism in modern society, particularly as modernity is epitomized in North American (Canada and United States) and Western European contexts. We then explore ways hunting may contribute to linking modern society and food production. Our analysis tracks hunting through the practices of searching, killing, processing, and consuming food. Along the way, we highlight how tensions associated with technology, both formal and informal social control, and commoditization may constrain the potential hunting holds for making linkages between human and natural systems explicit.

Social and Political Context

As part of the social, cultural, and material transformation of society often referred to as modernity, nature has gradually become objectified and separated from humans. Institutional transformations accompanying industrialization, the scientific and technological revolution, and neoliberal economic systems have given us a nature that is presumed measurable and controllable. According to [Karl] Marx, the production within capitalist modernity conceals all social relations and represents them as relations between material things. Marx labels this phenomenon commodity fetishism. [B.] Elling argues that Marx's identification of commodities as the core element of the economy and the real product of labor denotes the central abstraction of modernity. The food we perceive as real, therefore, is that which magically appears before us—flavorful, colorful, nutritious, and devoid of connection with labor.

Hunting provides an opportunity to link modern humans with natural systems through their food, and is a global phenomenon to which nearly every human culture can trace its roots. Here, we focus on Western European and North American contexts. These regions include modern nations where hunting is a culturally important activity associated with food production for millions of participants with diverse socioeconomic backgrounds.

In 2007, Ireland topped the European nations in terms of hunting participation with 9% of the population participating. In Nordic countries, about 4% of the total population hunts. France (2.1%), Spain (2.3%), Portugal (2.3%), and Greece (2.7%) also host large hunting populations. Less than 2% of the population hunts in most of the remaining European nations including Germany (0.4%). In the United States, there are approximately 12.5 million hunters, constituting ~4% of the total population, and 5.1% of Canadians hunt (1996 national survey Importance of Nature to Canadians; http://www.ec.gc.ca/nature). The significance of these numbers should be interpreted within the demographic profile of each nation. In Denmark, for example, although only 3.3% of the population hunts, that number translates into greater than 5% of the population that is eligible to hunt (older than 15 years). Although a decline in proportion of the population that hunts occurred in many nations during the last years of the 20th Century, hunting remains a widespread activity in many highly industrial and postindustrial regions of the world, and participation has remained more stable than for many other forms of nature-based recreation. In these societies, hunting is shifting from a life supporting activity of rural communities to a leisure activity of increasingly urbanized populations. Indigenous peoples provide small, but notable exceptions to these trends.

Hunting presents an intriguing opportunity for linking modern society with natural systems because the symbolic meaning of food nurtured by hunting is rooted in pre-modern materiality.

Research on the social aspects of hunting typically examines hunting as a set of practices involved in (1) searching for game animals, (2) killing those animals, and (3) processing and consuming game. Although many hunters are keenly interested in the political, legal, and technological ramifications of their avocation, this interest is not as fundamental as the search for game animals, and if the search is successful, killing, and then processing and consuming animals. Our analysis of hunting in this essay is limited to these practices. We rely on neo-Marxist and Durkheimian perspectives to critically analyze how hunting may render connections between human and natural systems explicitly visible, and then nurture a totemic meaning for food connected to natural systems.

The exploitation of nature and human laborers associated with food production has been widely critiqued within the sociology of agriculture. Some scholars explore ways to awaken consumers to the intricacies of food production by studying and reproducing the material, economic, and production conditions hiding behind this commodity. Others examine how the symbolic meaning of food interacts with consumption and consumers' attempts to shape society. The first stream of research is grounded in Marx's critique of political economy, the second in [Emile] Durkheim's theory of ritual.

Hunting and Connection

From Marx, we draw on the claim that value inheres to commodities themselves, rather than being derived from the labor, raw materials, and instruments used to produce those commodities. From Durkheim, we draw the concept of totemism, or society's tendency to confer sacredness on certain objects, and then use those totems to imbue other objects (often commodities) with social significance. Most relevant for our analysis is the idea that totemic meaning often generates intense social cohesion at the same time it builds a sense of connectedness between the social group and those objects that have become totemic. Because human society cannot help but employ totems in connection to basic needs, it generates totemic meaning for food. Hunting offers an increasingly rare means to connect that totemic meaning to natural systems.

Hunting presents an intriguing opportunity for linking modern society with natural systems because the symbolic meaning of food nurtured by hunting is rooted in pre-modern materiality instead of late (or post) modernity, as is the case with movements such as fair trade, slow food, and organic food. Hunting, however, faces the same threat of neo-liberal cooptation as other social activities. The lively debate within hunting culture regarding whether privatized wildlife count as wild game, for example, suggests a collision between a pre-modern culture intensely connected to nature and a modern culture bent on privatization and commoditization.

Through the practices of searching, killing, processing and consuming wildlife, hunting has the potential to link humans with natural processes and objects imprecated in food production.

Our dual focus on North America and Western Europe facilitates an international comparison across cultures where food commoditization faces disparate consumer and producer actions (e.g., U.S. patenting and use of genetically modified organisms without labeling versus European rejection of many genetically modified foods and requiring those that are accepted to be labeled) and where hunting faces different political and social challenges. In both North America and Western Europe, wildlife generally is perceived as a public good that is held in trust by relevant governments. Similarly, whether on state lands or on private property, hunting is subject to management and regulation by those same governments.

Other than migratory game birds, hunting regulations in Canada and the United States are developed and managed at the provincial/state/territorial, rather than the national, level. In regions of the United States and Canada where public land predominates, hunting opportunities are broadly available and relatively inexpensive for local residents, and can be purchased by visitors for additional licensing fees. In regions of the United States where private land predominates, however, people typically must also pay property owners for access to the land (or hunting lease) before they can hunt.

In Nordic countries including Sweden, Norway, and Finland the freedom to roam or "all man's right" gives the public rights to hike, camp, pick berries, and observe wildlife on private property. This generally also includes limited rights to small game hunting. Large game hunting occurs on both state and private lands subject to a variety of individual and community-level arrangements. These rights were recently formalized into law (e.g., Norway's Outdoor Recreation Act [1957]). Hunting on the European continent shares more similarities with private land regions of the United States, where the most significant costs for hunters are payments that must be made to private land owners. In sum, there is an array of ways that hunters can legally access hunting grounds within these modern societies, depending on state, provincial, national, and other regulations as well as societal norms.

Hunting and Modernity

This essay was motivated by the idea that alienation between humans and nature is one of the most basic obstacles to sustainability. Food production and consumption provides one repetitive dynamic rooted in nature that can highlight linkages between human and natural systems. The sustainable food movement has struggled to unveil the material conditions of food production and help consumers recognize the role of nature in the food they eat. The organic food sector, however, has been criticized for attributing an artificially harmonious totemic significance to organic food that masks, rather than grows out of, the material conditions of organic farming. Critics cite incongruous practices such as abusive labor conditions, destruction of wildlife habitat, and excessive use of fossil fuels in production and transportation.

Food produced via hunting offers an alternative approach to linking humans with nature. Through the practices of searching, killing, processing and consuming wildlife, hunting has the potential to link humans with natural processes and objects imprecated in food production. As with other cultural practices, however, hunting remains susceptible to the modern tendency to position humans as separate and dominant over other beings in order to achieve the illusion of control. Significant modernistic incursions into hunting culture occur in the form of technology, social control, and commoditization. Realization of hunting's potential to highlight linkages between human and natural systems depends largely on the ability of hunting culture to balance on the edge of modernity and pre-modernity.

Despite its positive associations with conservation, hunting's cultural contributions may be even more valuable.

Hunting maintains and communicates the experience and associated knowledge of providing food in a practical way that also exceeds instrumental logic. One of its most valuable and unappreciated contributions is unmasking the hidden kill that modern society demands. It does this by making it difficult for people to completely ignore the ways life uses death to perpetuate itself. Realizing hunting's conciliatory potential requires hunting culture to iteratively embrace its ambiguous relationship with modernity: it responds to the late modern desire for local and free range food, while simultaneously reversing the modern tendency to mask death from public view. Further, although they cannot completely reject those counter-potential elements we have identified as technology, social control, and commoditization, hunters must struggle to avoid the loss of hunting's pre-modern legacy. We see this as an explicitly political problem.

Hunting culture has begun the political task of recognizing and framing itself as a significant contributor to sustainability by explicitly highlighting its role in the production of local and free range food. Pressured by a significant and vocal public opposition to hunting in northern Europe, for example, hunting associations in Sweden, Norway, Finland, Denmark, and Iceland, have developed an ethical and social awareness of the broader social potential to link society with natural systems, as well as an awareness of the internal ambiguities existing within the hunting culture. This awareness is materialized in a text addressed primarily to transnational political institutions of Europe. The text formulates an identity for Nordic hunting culture that describes hunting as an activity for everyone. It focuses on hunting's connection to food production and its contributions to sustainability, describing practices and experiences that allow hunters to share connections with nature with society. By emphasizing those elements, the text positions the Nordic Hunters' Cooperation as a counterweight to some of the modernistic incursions that threaten to undermine hunting's potential to reconnect humans with natural systems. However, communicating this social identity on a political level does not in itself prevent ongoing structural changes, such as privatization and commoditization, which constrain hunting's potential to make these connections.

Hunting and Sustainability

Hunting has long been recognized as an adjunct to conservation and sustainability. In the United States, for example, the CP-33-Habitat Buffers for Upland Birds program within the Conservation Reserve Program involves paying landowners to manage their field borders for northern bobwhite (a highly prized game species among hunters). Collateral benefits of the program include reduction of soil erosion and runoff of agricultural chemicals and improved conditions for many songbird species that rely on early successional habitat. Modern hunting is arguably the most sustainable form of food production in the history of humanity. With few exceptions (e.g., food plots planted to attract game animals) producing food via hunting equates to protecting productive and threatened ecosystems (e.g., bottomland hardwoods, wetlands), thus creating natural and free range food. Hunting may actually be more "cruelty free" than industrial agriculture where one pass (multiple passes typically occur) of agricultural machinery over a field kills more animals (e.g., field mice, ground nesting birds) per gram of vegetable protein produced than hunting. Further, all forms of agriculture (including organic and sustainable versions) kill some wild animals indirectly by dictating agricultural land uses in areas that could be habitat.

Despite its positive associations with conservation, hunting's cultural contributions may be even more valuable. Hunting offers a realistic means to highlight connections between humans and other living beings by linking modern society with natural systems. Through engagement in the practices of searching, killing, processing, and consuming, hunters offer society opportunities to remember humanity's complex interdependence with other living creatures.

Faroe Islands Whale Hunting Does Little Harm

Tim Ecott

Tim Ecott is a journalist who contributes to the BBC and numerous other media organizations and publications. He is the author of the memoir Stealing Water.

In Tórshavn, capital of the Faroe Islands, I met a man who first helped his father kill a whale with a sharp knife when he was eight years old. The spouting blood soaked his hair and covered his face like warpaint. He remembered the warmth on his skin, a contrast to the cold North Atlantic in which they stood.

Non-Human Persons

These days we assume that people who kill whales and dolphins must be bad. Flipper and his cousins are our friends, and notwithstanding that unfortunate business with Moby-Dick, those who pursue whales for their flesh must be terrible human beings. We know now, as Herman Melville did not, that cetaceans are exceptional mammals, highly intelligent with elaborate social networks and close family relationships. They are capable of exhibiting grief and even of coming to the aid of human beings in distress.

In several parts of the world, there are moves to give these special animals legal protection as 'non-human persons.' India passed that law late last year, and in 2011 the American Association for the Advancement of Science began gathering support for the Declaration of Rights for Cetaceans. The first article in that declaration is: 'Every individual cetacean has the right to life.'

In a week or two, environmental campaigners from Sea Shepherd will be touring Britain enlisting public support to end what they call the 'barbaric and merciless slaughter of whales and dolphins in the Faroe Islands.' The campaign is gathering rapid traction on social media, and video clips of the Faroese hunt (known as the *grindadráp*) have been 'liked' and circulated in their hundreds of thousands. In those clips, the sea is stained red, the flapping pilot whales are dragged ashore with ropes and grappling hooks, and they are killed with a sharp instrument that severs the spine close to the head, resulting in almost instantaneous death.

According to the North Atlantic Marine Mammal Conservation Organisation, pilot whales number more than 750,000, and each year the slaughter is estimated to take less than 0.1 per cent of the population.

Sea Shepherd compares the Faroese whale hunt with the Japanese dolphin slaughter at Taiji, an annual process where hundreds of dolphins are herded into a small rocky cove. Babies and young adults are then separated from their mothers for sale to Chinese theme parks, and the others are stabbed to death by fishermen from above with flensing knives attached to bamboo poles. It is an awful scene of prolonged carnage. And, as we know, Japan has been utterly unwilling to countenance restrictions on its annual so-called 'scientific whaling' expeditions.

I respect the bravery with which Sea Shepherd confronts the Japanese whaling ships in the South Atlantic. And I applaud *Blackfish*, the recent documentary shining a spotlight on the highly dubious practice of exhibiting orcas for family entertainment at Seaworld in the USA. I've never killed a whale. And I think I could not do it. But I am uneasy about the campaign to target the Faroese and I'd defend the right of that father and his young son to hunt and kill whales. Theirs is a dramatic land, a green and treeless collection of 18 islands in the North Sea where just 50,000 people still live a life intimately connected to the elements. They have traditionally eaten puffins, great skuas, storm petrels and fulmars. Along the sharp sheer cliff edges there are wooden stakes embedded in the ground to which hardy islanders attach a rope and dangle perilously to catch birds on the wing, or gather eggs from nests on the rock face.

Wouldn't it be better if high-profile marine campaigns left the Faroese alone and focused on the more immediate and pressing threats to ocean ecosystems?

Twelve Hundred Years

Historically, the islanders have relied on whale meat as an essential part of their survival. These are fiercely independent people, intimately connected to their natural environment in spite of modern heating, air links (when the clouds clear for long enough) and the internet.

They have never set out to look for pilot whales: they kill them only when a school is discovered close to shore, and only if one of a small number of designated beaches is near enough to use as a landing ground. According to the North Atlantic Marine Mammal Conservation Organisation, pilot whales number more than 750,000, and each year the slaughter is estimated to take less than 0.1 per cent of the population. Records have been kept since 1584—which makes this the longest recorded tradition of any human-animal interaction. Experts think the practice has been going on for more than 1,200 years.

The *grindadráp* (whale hunt) is not merely something from the Faroese past. It is a reminder of their relationship to the sea, and the meat is still a favourite delicacy.

Focus Elsewhere

Wouldn't it be better if high-profile marine campaigns left the Faroese alone and focused on the more immediate and pressing threats to ocean ecosystems? Only this week a factory was discovered in Pu Qi in China that is processing more than 600 whale sharks a year. The world's largest fish, a harmless plankton feeder, is known to be dwindling fast across the tropics. In the Mediterranean, a combination of vested interests (some criminal) and lax European Union laws have resulted in the decimation of tuna populations. In the St Lawrence River in Canada, a small population of beluga whales is being poisoned by PCBs. Around 100 million sharks of all species are being caught worldwide to feed the Asian market for sharkfin soup. In many areas, 90 per cent of large carnivorous sharks have been removed from the ecosystem. In India and Sri Lanka, there is a burgeoning fishery for giant manta ray gills to make 'blood purifiers' for the Chinese medicine trade. Parrotfish and conch are being overfished in the Caribbean, allowing algae to lay waste to the coral reefs. The list could go on and on and on.

Endangered fish species are commonly found on most British restaurant tables and, due to overfishing, our once superabundant cod populations continue to show little sign of recovery. These are the marine issues that I worry about. There is one ocean on our planet, not six or seven or more according to labels on a chart. All that sea is connected to form a giant system that we have neglected and continue to plunder. Let's not victimise one tiny human population who are carrying on a tradition that will in all probability die out naturally in time. For now, let them eat whales.

Fox Hunting Helps Manage Wildlife

Jim Barrington

Jim Barrington is a former executive director of the League Against Cruel Sports who has been involved in animal welfare issues for nearly forty years. He is now an animal welfare consultant to the Countryside Alliance, Council of Hunting Associations, and the All Party Parliamentary Middle Way Group, all located in the United Kingdom.

Recent parliamentary questions indicate that the issue of hunting with dogs has never really gone away. It seems that the Hunting Act [of 2004, which banned many kinds of hunting with dogs in England], far from putting this matter to bed, has just kept fanning the flames.

Dogs and Wildlife Management

So it might be an opportune time to examine a few factors behind one of the most controversial pieces of legislation passed in recent years. The whole anti-hunting case appears to be based more on perceptions and public opinion polls, rather than hard evidence of cruelty.

To argue that the dog, which is staggeringly helpful to humans in so many ways—search and rescue dogs, guide dogs, hearing dogs, dogs for the disabled, guard dogs, police dogs, drug sniffer dogs, explosive sniffer dogs, herding dogs, dogs that can detect cancer—cannot be used in wildlife management is sheer nonsense. Scenting hounds generally [catch] the old, weak, sick and injured quarry and importantly there is no wounding; the animal is either killed or escapes unscathed. To argue in some pseudo moral way that repeal of the Hunting Act is a backward step, as some do, shows a fundamental ignorance of life in the wild.

The argument that hunting is supposedly insignificant in managing the fox population, as claimed by the anti-hunting groups, once again fails to understand that as a wildlife management process, it is not about the numbers killed, but the health and reduced level of the population left alive that is important.

Therefore, to liken hunting with hounds to dog fighting and badger baiting, as recent public opinion polls have done, and to imply that these obscenities might be legalised not only grossly distorts the practice of hunting in the minds of those questioned, but is also done precisely to achieve the desired result.

Another argument points to the success of the Hunting Act, claiming 280 prosecutions. True numerically, but not true if you think all these cases were against hunts. The vast majority are for poaching, which of course was already against the law.

Banning Hunting Hurts Animals

Here is a genuine fact. For all the millions of pounds spent on campaigning in support of the Hunting Act, not one penny has been spent by any anti-hunting group to assess the effect this law has had on wildlife. These organisations rely on another fact, which is that most people do not understand the complex practice of hunting with hounds and will not examine the unprincipled, illogical and badly drafted Hunting Act. The limited research that has been undertaken indicates that the Hunting Act has been detrimental to animal welfare.

Of course any method of wildlife management, whether it be hunting, shooting, game-keeping etc., can go wrong through bad practice or just sheer callousness. The way to resolve this is by way of a new wild mammals welfare law that would address such situations and any accusations of causing unnecessary suffering would then be tested in court on the basis of evidence, rather than prejudice or ignorance. This is the principle on which domestic animal cruelty cases are based and there is no reason why it should not apply to wild animals, given the different circumstances that wild animals live in compared to that of domestic animals. A further fact: the anti-hunting groups do not support such a law simply because this would make the Hunting Act redundant.

Some of the anti-hunting groups are charities, which are supposed to base their policies and public statements on firm evidence, something that has clearly not happened in the hunting debate.

Despite claiming scientific evidence to support a hunting ban, no research has been forthcoming. The anti-hunting organisations, being more obsessed with banning hunting than improving animal welfare, know that proving hunting to be cruel in a court of law is problematic and consequently they oppose a far better wild animal welfare law.

On an equally serious point, some of the anti-hunting groups are charities, which are supposed to base their policies and public statements on firm evidence, something that has clearly not happened in the hunting debate. This slide reflects a wider situation that has deteriorated over decades, resulting in the Public Accounts Committee saying in February 2014: "We are therefore dismayed to report yet again that the Charity Commission continues to perform poorly and is still failing to regulate charities effectively. The Commission is a reactive rather than proactive regulator, and has yet to use its powers properly in registering, monitoring, or intervening in charities."

The government is currently reviewing the role of the Charity Commission and considering strengthening its powers.

The present situation has allowed some charities to persuade the public and certain gullible politicians that a ban on hunting is of benefit to wildlife, based on nothing more than their opinion, propaganda and a few dodgy polls. This is not the proper role of a charity and ironically and sadly, in deviating from that path, they now stand in the way of genuinely improving wild animal welfare.

CHAPTER 4

Does Using Animals for Entertainment Violate Their Rights?

Chapter Preface

Exotic pets are animals that are generally thought of as wild and are not usually domesticated. Examples of exotic pets include big cats like lions and tigers, large snakes like boa constrictors, coyotes, or raccoons.

No one is exactly sure how many exotic pets are kept in the United States. The animal rights organization Born Free USA says that there are "millions of wild animals, including reptiles, large felines, nonhuman primates, and others" kept as pets in the United States.[1] According to Chelsea Whyte, writing in *New Scientist*, the World Wildlife Federation estimates that there are more than four thousand tigers kept as pets in the United States, which is more than the thirty-two hundred tigers who live in the wild worldwide.[2]

There are a number of problems with keeping exotic pets. As Jodi Kendall points out in *National Geographic*, wild animals have special needs and requirements that can be very difficult to deal with in a home.[3] Tigers roam large territories and may not get enough exercise or space in a house or enclosed yard. Wild animals are also strong and some can jump or climb to great heights. It may be difficult to keep them contained—and they can endanger others if they escape, as when two chimpanzees escaped a home and attacked cars in Las Vegas in 2012.

1. Born Free USA, "Ten Fast Facts About Exotic 'Pets,'" n.d. (accessed July 18, 2014). http://www.bornfreeusa.org/facts.php?p=439&more=1.

2. Chelsea Whyte, "Exotic Pets USA: Tigers, Big Bucks and Organised Crime," *New Scientist*, October 21, 2011. http://www.newscientist.com/article/dn21078-exotic-pets -usa-tigers-big-bucks-and-organised-crime.html#.VKFxR6d_Y.

3. Jodi Kendall, "Wild at Home: Exotic Animals as Pets," *National Geographic*, n.d. (accessed July 18, 2014). http://channel.nationalgeographic.com/wild/animal -intervention/articles/wild-at-home-exotic-animals-as-pets.

People will sometimes buy exotic animals as infants and then discover that the pets are too difficult to control as they turn from cute cubs into three hundred pound tigers, or transform from tiny slithering friends into giant twenty-foot pythons. According to Born Free USA, animals may be abandoned as they grow, which can endanger people or result in the animals' deaths. Similarly, if owners fail in care, the animals may be hurt; one of the chimps who escaped in 2012 in Las Vegas was shot and killed.

Despite these issues, some individuals still argue that people should be allowed to own exotic pets. Zuzana Kukol, president of Responsible Exotic Animal Ownership (REXANO), maintains that the dangers in owning an exotic animal are low:

> On average in the United States, only 3.25 people per year are killed by captive big cats, snakes, elephants and bears. Most of these fatalities are owners, family members, friends and trainers voluntarily on the property where the animals were kept. Meanwhile, traffic accidents kill about 125 people per day.[4]

Kukol adds that most owners are responsible and that their freedom to have the pet of their choice should not be infringed.

The remainder of this chapter looks at issues surrounding animal rights in other situations in which animals are used for entertainment, such as zoos, circuses, or racing.

---

4. Zuzana Kukol, "Opposing View: Let People Own Exotic Animals," *USA Today*, October 20, 2011. http://usatoday30.usatoday.com/news/opinion/story/2011-10-20/own -exotic-animals-Ohio/50846342/1.

Zoos Are Cruel and Unnecessary

Liz Tyson, interviewed by Earth Times

Liz Tyson is the director of the Captive Animals' Protection Society.

*E*arth Times: *With the internet, as well as DVDs, 3D TV, etc., are zoos really necessary to teach people about animals in the 21st century?*

Liz Tyson: Not at all. As you quite rightly mention, there is a wealth of information out there which someone who is interested in learning about wildlife can access at the touch of a button. I think it is important to note though that literature, film, television and the internet are not *alternatives* to learning about animals because zoos have never been necessary for education. The educative message delivered by zoos is, at best, distorted and, at worst, damaging to the cause that the zoos purport to champion—that is; the conservation of species.

Zoos Show Animals Out of Context

By showing a tiger in a cage to a child, a zoo can teach that child nothing more than the size of a tiger, the colour of a tiger and the shape of a tiger. A zoo shows the animal completely out of context, outside of its natural habitat and the ecosystem it was designed to inhabit.

The message that the child takes away with them is: if you ever want to see a tiger, come to the zoo, where we can show you one at your convenience. What it fails to demonstrate to the child [is] the urgency of the need for habitat conservation, or the complexity of the role of the tiger in its natural habitat, or the ways in which that child could aid the conservation of the species in reality. If the zoo attempts to explain these factors then it can only do so by providing written information, or perhaps audio visual material. As such, the important messages are delivered via mediums that the child could access without ever setting foot in a zoo and the presence of the tiger becomes irrelevant.

Worryingly, zoos teach children that humans can control nature. They demonstrate that if an irreplaceable natural habitat is destroyed by our actions, we can pluck individual animals out of the destruction, manipulate their breeding cycle and produce more of them to live in city centre zoos or safari parks thereby "saving" the species. In my opinion, the idea of future generations buying into this premise is a very frightening prospect.

What are the differences between "good zoos" and "bad zoos"?

Whilst we are fundamentally against the keeping of animals in captivity for entertainment, it would be wrong to deny that some zoos are worse than others. Just last year, we carried out an investigation where the owner of a zoo sliced a growth off the face of one of the animals in its petting zoo with a penknife without any anaesthetic rather than take it to the vets. Another zoo we investigated feeds animals stale bread and cakes as the majority of their daily diet. Last year we also revealed that a large safari park kept its big cats locked in small and dilapidated enclosures for up to 18 hours a day.

Every single investigation our organisation has carried out into zoos has led to the exposure of serious issues; for the animals, the staff or the visitors. These zoos range from some of the country's biggest and longest-established to small set-ups where amateur animal collectors have turned their menageries into money-making ventures. As such, what may appear to be a "good zoo" on the surface, may prove to be something very different when you begin to dig deeper.

Notwithstanding this sliding scale of provision for the most basic needs of the animals, our organisation was founded upon the strong belief that the caging of any animal to fulfill our curiosity and for commercial gain has absolutely no place in modern society. Animals are not ours to control and imprison and as such, I agree that there are "bad zoos", I agree that there are "worse zoos" but I do not believe that there is such thing as a "good zoo".

I can say with great confidence that a zoo enclosure can never be a proper substitute for an animal's natural habitat.

No Substitute

Can artificial enclosures ever be a proper substitute for an animal's natural habitat?

I have been lucky enough to spend a number of years living in the Amazon rainforest as the early part of my career was spent working toward the conservation of neotropical primates. I don't think that it is possible to appreciate the enormity, the complexity and the diversity of an environment such as this without experiencing it first hand.

Having had the privilege of seeing troops of monkeys springing from tree to tree in complete freedom, having come across the paw print of a jaguar who had recently passed over the trail our group was walking, having seen a deadly snake devour a frog whole, having seen the enigmatic pink river dolphins rise up out of the river for air and having seen macaws flying high above the trees screeching at interlopers in defence of their territory, I can say with great confidence that a zoo enclosure can never be a proper substitute for an animal's natural habitat.

A number of strict standards are currently in place for zoos to adhere to. But what further improvements can still be made?

This is an area in which our organisation works on in detail and whilst there is legislation in place to impose standards in zoos, it is recognised that there are major concerns with regards to the enforcement of these standards. So serious are concerns about the alleged failure of local authorities to implement the terms of the Zoo Licensing Act 1981 that the government department responsible for the regime (Defra), currently has the system under review.

There are over 400 zoos in the UK [United Kingdom] alone, ranging from butterfly farms to menageries of 100 or so animals to the immense safari parks that have thousands of animals ranging across large areas of land. Many of the smaller zoos are exempt from the licensing standards and thus, are not subject to inspections. For the larger zoos, they are inspected once a year (at best) or once every three years (as a minimum). The inspection is carried out over a maximum of two working days and might have to assess hundreds or even thousands of animals. When you bear in mind that the inspectors also need to review record keeping, health and safety, procedures, education and conservation contribution in the allotted time, it becomes clear that, even with the best of intentions, the system is simply unworkable.

Subjecting an animal to a lifetime of captivity, whether to inspire a passion for conservation or to entertain are two sides of the same coin.

When we consider that the Zoo Licensing Act was introduced 30 years ago, and it is still not working, we would argue that rather than look to improve this ailing regime to maintain the status quo and legitimise zoos, we should agree [on] a point where we accept that the animals in zoos are not protected by legislation and work to phase out the industry.

Other Ways to Inspire

Do zoo visits really inspire a passion for conservation, or are they merely passive entertainment?

It is impossible to say what zoos inspire in other people—I am sure that for some people they do inspire passion in the same way they provoke sadness or anger in others. I think the overriding point here is that, even if they did inspire a passion for conservation, the end does not justify the means. Subjecting an animal to a lifetime of captivity, whether to inspire a passion for conservation or to entertain are two sides of the same coin. One motivation may be seen as more acceptable from a societal point of view but the situation of the tiger pacing up and down in his enclosure day-in day-out remains the same regardless of the motivation of the zoo owners.

I have been lucky enough to work with a number of great educators over the years whose professional motivation is centred around inspiring a passion for conservation. They work in weird and wonderful ways and use a huge variety of methods to educate, inform and entertain audiences of all ages. Using song, dance, poetry, theatre, debate, field trips, workshops, arts and crafts, video and internet and literature amongst a great number of other methods, these imaginative people are changing people's perceptions on a daily basis. If the motivation of zoo owners was truly to inspire passion for conservation then, with a little imagination, they could begin to lead the way out of this archaic practice and towards a learning experience which was both valuable and, most importantly, free of suffering.

Ringling Brothers Circus's Treatment of Elephants Is Cruel

Deborah Nelson

Deborah Nelson is a journalist on the faculty of the University of Maryland. She is the author of The War Behind Me: Vietnam Veterans Confront the Truth About U.S. War Crimes.

It was a drizzly winter day, and inside the Jacksonville Coliseum, Kenny, a three-year-old Asian elephant, was supposed to perform his usual adorable tricks in The Greatest Show on Earth: identifying the first letter of the alphabet by kicking a beach ball marked with an "A," twirling in a tight circle, perching daintily atop a tub, and, at the end of his act, waving farewell to the audience with a handkerchief grasped in his trunk.

A Sick Elephant

But Kenny was clearly sick. Elephants are highly intelligent creatures that develop at a similar rate as humans. In the wild, Kenny would still be at his mother's side, just beginning to wean. In captivity, he was a voracious consumer of water and hay but for the past day or so had showed little interest in either. He seemed listless. Worried attendants in the tent where the elephants were chained between shows twice alerted a circus veterinary technician.

Under federal regulations, sick elephants must get prompt medical care and a veterinarian's okay before performing. Neither occurred, and at showtime Kenny trotted out to the center ring. He developed diarrhea during the morning show. During the afternoon performance, he began bleeding from his bottom and afterward struggled to stay on his feet. It was only then that Gary D. West, a circus veterinarian, arrived from St. Petersburg to examine the young elephant. West prescribed antibiotics and recommended that Kenny skip the evening show—in a later affidavit, he didn't stress concern for the elephant's health but rather that "he might pass some blood which might be seen by a spectator and cause speculation as to his well being."

West was overruled by Gunther Gebel-Williams, Ringling Bros. and Barnum & Bailey's legendary golden-haired animal tamer who'd retired from the ring to be vice president of animal care. So Kenny made his third appearance, although he was too weak to perform any stunts.

After the evening show, the bleeding continued. The elephant crew gave Kenny rehydration fluids and shackled him in his stall. Less than two hours later, a night attendant discovered his bloodied body on the concrete floor. The cause of death remains unclear.

Feld Entertainment, Ringling's corporate parent, did not announce Kenny's death to the public for nearly a week, until an employee tipped off animal rights activists. They demanded action from the Department of Agriculture, which licenses and inspects circuses under the Animal Welfare Act. Under intense public pressure, including a letter-writing campaign headlined by [actor] Kim Basinger, the USDA charged Feld Entertainment with two willful violations for making Kenny perform ill without prompt or adequate veterinary care.

In one notable instance, documents came to light only after a judge threatened to put Feld executives in jail.

A Turning Point?

That was in 1998, and at the time it seemed like a turning point in the decades-long fight over circus elephants. For years, animal rights organizations had been releasing horrific undercover videos showing Ringling trainers abusing elephants, but USDA investigations never produced evidence that officials deemed strong enough to warrant action. Now there was a dead body—and a recent precedent. The agency had just fined the King Royal Circus, a small family operation, $200,000 for allowing an elephant to die in an overheated trailer of an untreated salmonella infection.

But after a few months, the USDA announced a settlement. Feld Entertainment would donate $20,000 to elephant causes. In return, the agency absolved the company of blame for Kenny's death and further declared, "Ringling Bros. has never been adjudged to have violated the [Animal Welfare Act]."

The USDA unwittingly opened a new chapter in the animal rights movement. Frustrated by the agency's inaction, advocates turned to the federal courts. This shift in strategy has not yet produced a judgment against Feld Entertainment, but it has unearthed an extraordinary trove of records that its lawyers and government regulators had taken great pains to ensure the public would never see; in one notable instance, documents came to light only after a judge threatened to put Feld executives in jail. They include dozens of videos and thousands of pages of investigation files, veterinary records, circus train logs, and courtroom testimony.

Feld Entertainment is a privately held corporation owned by Kenny's namesake, CEO Kenneth Feld, whose family bought Ringling for more than $8 million in 1967 and folded it into an entertainment empire that includes Ringling's three year-round touring circus troupes, as well as Disney On Ice, Disney Live, and Monster Jam. Together these shows play for more than 30 million people a year, with annual revenues estimated at between $500 million and $1 billion. But the four-ton behemoths are the biggest draw, generating more than $100 million annually in revenues, according to testimony by Feld executives.

Pampered Performers

It's hard not to be captivated. Elephants are smart, social creatures that communicate through a complex score of rumbles, trumpets, and gestures; they also have long memories and the capacity to celebrate, mourn, and empathize.

Feld Entertainment portrays its population of some 50 endangered Asian elephants as "pampered performers" who "are trained through positive reinforcement, a system of repetition and reward that encourages an animal to show off its innate athletic abilities." But a yearlong *Mother Jones* investigation shows that Ringling elephants spend most of their long lives either in chains or on trains, under constant threat of the bullhook, or ankus—the menacing tool used to control elephants. They are lame from balancing their 8,000-pound frames on tiny tubs and from being confined in cramped spaces, sometimes for days at a time. They are afflicted with tuberculosis and herpes, potentially deadly diseases rare in the wild and linked to captivity. Barack, a calf born on the eve of the president's inauguration, had to leave the tour in February for emergency treatment of herpes—the second time in a year. Since Kenny's death, 3 more of the 23 baby elephants born in Ringling's vaunted breeding program have died, all under disturbing circumstances that weren't fully revealed to the public.

None of [the evidence of elephant abuse] has moved regulators to action.

Despite years of denials, Kenneth Feld has now admitted under oath that his trainers routinely "correct" elephants by hitting them with bullhooks, whipping them, and on occasion using electric prods. He even admitted to witnessing it.

But perhaps more disturbing still is the government's failure to act. Since Kenny's death, the USDA has conducted more than a dozen investigations of Feld Entertainment. Inspectors have found baby elephants injured and bound at Ringling's Center for Elephant Conservation in Florida. Whistleblowers have stepped forward with harrowing accounts of beatings. Activists have released even more videos of elephant abuse, and local humane authorities have documented wounds and lameness.

None of that has moved regulators to action.

Circus oversight rests with the animal care unit in the USDA's Animal and Plant Health Inspection Service [APHIS]. Officials there, as at Feld Entertainment, were not willing to be interviewed. So I called W. Ron DeHaven, who headed the animal care unit from 1996 until 2001 before ascending to lead all of APHIS from 2004 to 2007. (He is now executive vice president of the American Veterinary Medical Association.)

During DeHaven's tenure at the USDA, a 2005 audit by the department's inspector general criticized the animal care unit for being too lenient on violators. The report singled out the Eastern region, which oversees Ringling's operations, for its failure "to take enforcement action against violators who compromised public safety or animal health."

With an annual budget of only $16 million and 111 employees to monitor nearly 9,000 animal entertainment, breeding, and research facilities, the agency didn't have the capacity to prosecute many cases, DeHaven explained. He acted on the egregious cases, he said, like King Royal. I asked what made that case worse than others. A dead elephant, he said, and a clear violation.

Taking on Feld

How was that different than Kenny? DeHaven said he didn't recall the particulars of that case. But, he added, "You don't take on an organization like Feld Entertainment without having strong evidence to support it."

That sentiment was echoed by Kenneth H. Vail, who for decades served as the USDA's lead legal counsel on animal welfare cases. We met at his red brick townhouse in northwest DC in July, just after his retirement. Thin-faced, with soft eyes and a quiet voice, he invited me in out of the 100-degree heat to talk for more than an hour. He said Feld Entertainment cases received special attention from him and other top department brass. "A case involving a multimillion-dollar company is significant," Vail said. "There's a political aspect to Feld cases. The company is a big target for animal rights groups." True, USDA investigators advocated action against Feld Entertainment on numerous occasions, but Vail said he never felt their evidence could withstand a legal challenge by the company. "There's no way to control an elephant without an ankus," and the Animal Welfare Act doesn't prohibit it, he explained. Maybe a time will come when bullhooks, chains, and "elephants getting paraded around doing unnatural things" is prohibited, he said, but until then, litigating abuse is difficult.

[Feld Entertainment] poured tens of millions of dollars into PR campaigns that portrayed the elephants as willing performers, as well as legal firepower to keep regulators and activists at bay.

"If I were an elephant, I wouldn't want to be with Feld Entertainment," Vail conceded. "It's a tough life." . . .

The Problem of Animal Rights

By the time Irvin Feld died in 1984, leaving his son, Kenneth, to run the [Ringling Bros.] show, animal rights organizations were proliferating. Zoos began adopting an emerging animal management philosophy called "protected contact," which controls animals with physical barriers instead of sticks and chains. But this was of little use to the circus, where direct interaction between humans and wild beasts is the point. Feld

Entertainment faced a conundrum: The audiences still wanted to see elephants—but they wanted to see them treated nicely.

So the company poured tens of millions of dollars into PR campaigns that portrayed the elephants as willing performers, as well as legal firepower to keep regulators and activists at bay. [Trainer Gunther] Gebel-Williams got a makeover. A press release lauded his "animal training based on mutual respect and positive reinforcement" that "forever changed the standards of animal training." It's true that Gebel-Williams had an extraordinary rapport with the animals, but it's also true that he routinely whipped elephants and struck them with bullhooks. A few months after Kenny's death, Gebel-Williams was spotted whipping a baby elephant in the face outside a circus train in Mexico City.

Nonetheless, the sleight of hand worked. When Gebel-Williams died in 2001, the *Sarasota Herald-Tribune*'s obituary noted that he had "substituted humane, positive reinforcement and reward for the fear and force upon which many animal trainers rely."

The biggest challenge for Feld Entertainment's "positive reinforcement" campaign was the ubiquitous bullhook or ankus. It's a malevolent-looking instrument, about three feet long, with a sharp, metal point-and-hook combination at one end. The point is for pushing. The hook, inserted in the mouth or at the top of the ear, is for pulling. Both are sharp enough to pierce elephant hide. . . .

Feld Entertainment rebranded the ankus as a "guide." Handlers hid them in their sleeves or carried smaller, less menacing-looking models during the show. As Joan Galvin, the company's vice president, assured the Associated Press in 1998: "Elephants are one of the most beloved acts that perform in the circus today. Abusive techniques are absolutely prohibited."

Beatings

In December of that same year, two attendants on the Blue Unit left the tour during a stop in Huntsville, Alabama. They called a local animal welfare office, explaining they had quit in disgust over the way the elephants were treated. The woman put them in touch with Pat Derby, a former Hollywood trainer who had founded the Performing Animal Welfare Society (PAWS).

With fiery orange hair atop a stout physique, a gravel voice, and a talent for attention-grabbing tactics, Derby had been Ringling's No. 1 antagonist for more than a decade. Her supporters organized protests outside performances and shot videos of trainers hitting elephants.

Benjamin, a precocious three-year-old, also suffered frequent beatings from his trainer.

Derby arranged for lawyers to take the men's videotaped depositions and written affidavits. The attendants, Glenn Ewell and James Stechcon, had lived transient, sometimes troubled lives, working off and on for circuses. At Ringling, where they mucked out elephant pens and assisted with feeding, they claimed to have witnessed regular elephant abuse and more than a dozen extended beatings during their three months on the road.

Several of the beatings targeted Nicole, a twenty something-thing elephant named after Kenneth Feld's eldest daughter. Sweet-natured but clumsy, Nicole would frequently miss her cues to climb atop a tub and place her feet on the elephant next to her, Stechcon said in his videotaped statement. "I always rooted for her, 'Come on, Nicole, *get up*,'" he said. "But we left the show, brought the animals back to their area, and . . . we took the headpieces off, and as I was hanging them up, I heard the most horrible noise, just whack, whack, whack. I mean, really hard. It's hard to describe the noise. Like a baseball bat or something striking something not—not soft, and not hard . . . I turned around to look, and this guy was hitting her so fast and so hard [with the ankus], and sometimes he would take both hands and just really knock her, and he was just doing that. And I was, like, I couldn't believe it."

Benjamin, a precocious three-year-old, also suffered frequent beatings from his trainer, Ewell and Stechcon said. Able to balance on a wooden barrel, ride a tricycle, shoot hoops, play musical instruments, and paint a picture by holding a brush with his trunk, Benjamin had appeared on *The Today Show* and *CBS This Morning*. His trainer, Pat Harned, told journalists that Benjamin had been trained thanks to rewards of bread or bunches of bananas.

The whistleblowers told investigators that Harned also used force. "Pachyderms want to throw things on their back, it's a—it's a genetic response. Anyway, I saw Benjamin, after he was brushed off, take some sawdust and throw it on his back," Stechcon said. That upset Harned, who "dealt with it accordingly, with a bullhook, striking Benjamin all over the head, quite forcefully and repeatedly. It was not pretty."

Derby helped the men file a formal complaint to the USDA. In early January, a senior investigator and veterinarian followed up with a surprise visit to the Blue Unit, on tour near Miami. The USDA team found scars and abrasions on several elephants and a fresh puncture wound on another. Another Ringling employee reported treating hook boils—infected bullhook wounds—"twice a week on average."

But all five trainers and handlers named by Ewell and Stechcon denied abusing elephants or ever seeing anyone else do so. "I have a very good relationship with the elephants, especially the babies Benjamin and Shirley," Harned told the investigator. "There is no abuse of any of the elephants. I treat these elephants as my children."

DeHaven, the animal care unit director, received a report from the senior investigator that none of the allegations could be confirmed. But he also received a complaint from the director of the Eastern regional office about the quality of the investigation. She wrote that the investigator hadn't interviewed the Ringling employees whom the whistleblowers had identified as potential corroborating witnesses, nor had he followed upon the worrisome admission that hook boils were commonplace. . . .

Evidence [surfaced] that two Feld moles had infiltrated PAWS by posing as volunteers. . . . There was evidence of similar schemes against the People for the Ethical Treatment of Animals (PETA) and the Elephant Alliance.

Legal Efforts

By early 2000, Derby of PAWS had had enough. She turned to Katherine Meyer, a gregarious blonde who, with her husband, Eric Glitzenstein, ran what *Washingtonian* magazine called "the most effective public-interest law firm in Washington." The couple met working for Ralph Nader in the 1980s and, after striking out on their own in the 1990s, scored a string of animal rights victories that caught Derby's attention.

Meyer proposed that PAWS file a federal lawsuit against Feld Entertainment, seizing on a provision in the Endangered Species Act that allows citizens to sue violators directly. Such citizen lawsuits had been used to protect endangered animals in the wild but not in captivity. A win would revolutionize animal exhibits.

That same spring, two private detectives visited Derby. They explained that they'd been retained by a fired Feld executive to gather evidence of the company's illicit spying on animal rights groups. The former executive had reportedly stiffed them on their fee, so—for $200,000, records show—they offered up 20 boxes of documents on her organization. The materials included purloined records, weekly surveillance reports, and evidence that two Feld moles had infiltrated PAWS by posing as volunteers; one had gained entry to Derby's inner circle. There was evidence of similar schemes against the People for the Ethical Treatment of Animals (PETA) and the Elephant Alliance.

It was part of a multimillion-dollar spy operation run out of Feld headquarters to thwart and besmirch animal rights groups and others on the company's enemies list, according to a stunning *Salon* piece by Jeff Stein. Feld had even hired Clair George—the CIA's head of covert operations under President Reagan until his conviction for perjury in the Iran-Contra scandal. (George, who died in August, received a pardon from President George H.W. Bush.)

Derby filed a civil lawsuit against Feld Entertainment for racketeering and fraud on June 8, 2000, in the federal courthouse for the Eastern District of California. About a month later, Meyer filed the elephant lawsuit in the federal district courthouse in Washington, DC. Soon after, lawyers for Feld approached Derby with a generous settlement offer on the spy case. They would donate elephants and cash to her wildlife sanctuary if she dropped the elephant lawsuit and refrained from publicly criticizing Feld Entertainment. She agreed.

But the elephant lawsuit limped along with Meyer remaining lead counsel and Rider and seminal players in the animal rights movement—including the American Society for the Prevention of Cruelty to Animals, the Animal Welfare Institute, the Fund for Animals, and eventually the Animal Protection Institute—as plaintiffs. The case was assigned to US District Judge Emmet Sullivan, a mercurial jurist who quickly tossed the suit for lack of standing; he found that none of the *people* involved could prove that Feld Entertainment's actions had caused them harm. (Animals don't have standing.) The appeals court overruled him in 2003, at which point Meyer subpoenaed government documents and filed discovery requests with Feld Entertainment. Feld stalled for more than a year until the company's lawyers finally sent word that the records would be delivered on June 9, 2004.

Meyer prepared for a sizable document dump. But at the appointed hour the deliveryman left just two cardboard file boxes of press releases and other innocuous materials. Instead of the detailed veterinary charts Meyer had requested, she got a page or two on each elephant. She pressed, but Feld Entertainment stonewalled.

Meanwhile, the casualties at Ringling were mounting. In early August of 2004, an eight-month-old elephant named Riccardo was euthanized after he broke two legs. A Feld press release explained that he had been playing outside when he climbed, as he often did, onto "a round platform 19 inches high. This time, he lost his balance and fell." Although Ringling denied it, the activity sounded suspiciously like a training drill. Investigators recommended that Ringling be found in violation for failing to provide adequate care after he fell.

On August 20 and 21, an anti-cruelty activist in Oakland, California, videotaped a Ringling handler repeatedly striking a seven-year-old elephant with a bullhook while it was chained. It was Angelica, the same animal USDA inspectors discovered bound and injured at the Center for Elephant Conservation in 1999. This time, they recommended an $11,000 penalty for excessive force and chaining. A regional USDA director for animal care urged his superiors to take action: "Feld Entertainment is a large corporation with a previous enforcement history." Then-Illinois Sen. Barack Obama joined the chorus at PETA's request. The cases landed in Vail's office, where they hit a dead end.

Cruel? No, Elephants Love the Circus—And I Should Know, Says Dea Birkett, I Used to Ride Them in the Big Top

Dea Birkett

Dea Birkett is a former circus performer and a writer for The Guardian *and other publications.*

When I was a little girl, once a year, the park where I played on the seesaw and swings was transformed into a world of wondrous, exotic people and beasts.

I saw men walking on stilts and wobbling on a high wire, clowns squelching through custard pies, horses teetering on their hind legs and an elephant strolling around a sawdust ring. The circus had arrived.

So entranced was I by this spectacle that I resolved to run away and join the circus.

Most of all, I wanted to be an elephant girl. I longed to slide my hand over the deep ridges of the elephant's trunk, to feel the rhythm of its stride, to be transformed into the shimmering lady who smiled down from its back.

Well, it took me a good few years, but eventually I achieved my ambition and joined a circus in Italy when I was well into my 30s.

I was the oldest female in the troupe, with the exception of Julia—my elephant. But that did nothing to lessen my joy at being part of such an exotic world.

I would don my fishnet tights, twirl my tassels, adjust my feather head-dress and ride into the ring on Julia's back.

I thrilled to the roar of the crowd when Julia lifted her trunk while I teetered dangerously on her neck, waving and smiling.

I was reminded of those days by the news this week that the Great British Circus is about to embark on a nationwide tour—the first in the country in more than a decade to feature a performing elephant.

Predictably, the animal rights' activists have taken to their high-minded chariots and ridden into the ring.

The Born Free Foundation, a celebrity-studded animal welfare charity, wants the circus banned. They say performing elephants shouldn't be allowed because it's a form of cruelty.

Well, I don't agree because I have seen how the trainers tended their beloved animals.

Living on the road, we were often short of water and I would have to go without a good wash for a week—but Julia had a shower each morning, ready for the working day ahead.

When she wasn't performing, she wandered around the paddock with the five other elephants, knocking her trunk against the door of my 10ft trailer as if asking to come in.

In the next-door trailer, the couple with the dog act shared a bed with their puppies, breathing each others' air.

What's wrong with training animals to perform? It is no different from training a racehorse or teaching the family dog to respond to 'Sit!' at the kerb.

In the circus, the lives of the humans and the animals are completely entwined. No other people live so closely with the animals they care for. And it's the welfare of the animal performers, not the humans, that always comes first.

Julia hadn't been plucked from the jungle or captured in an elephant trap. Almost all circus animals are born in captivity. And many animals we think of as wild are considered domestic in the rest of the world.

In India, elephants are seen in the same way as we consider horses—they're working beasts.

And what's wrong with training animals to perform? It is no different from training a racehorse or teaching the family dog to respond to 'Sit!' at the kerb.

Animal behaviourist Dr Marthe Kiley-Worthington, who was commissioned by the RSPCA to report on animals in circuses, says many animals enjoy being taught tricks.

After 3,000 hours of scientific observation, she concluded it was wrong to assume animals should always be kept in a primitive, natural state.

Just as some human beings, such as athletes and circus artistes, enjoy tackling new physical skills, so do some animals. Even an old dog can learn new tricks.

Martin Lacey, owner and ringmaster of the Great British Circus, has worked with animals for more than 40 years, living with lions, tigers, camels and now an elephant.

Before the Born Free charity chased the circus out of town, he was presenting his big cat act as King Of The Cage.

I remember years ago going to see The One And Only Mr Martin Lacey and being entranced by the bow-tied, whiskered tamer in his scarlet jacket. Lacey and his big cats appeared on TV and made commercials.

His trailer, where he still spends nine months of the year, is hung with photographs, not of his children, but of his lions and tigers. His favourite feline companion was a lion called Kasanga.

'Kass was quite a character,' Lacey told me. 'He was always interested in anything that was going on.'

Kass and Martin were a team, a partnership. For the few winter months when the circus is off the road, he stays at home in Kasanga Manor in Lincolnshire, where his beloved Kass, who lived to 19, is buried in the garden.

Circus folk like Martin Lacey are the last of Britain's travelling players. If they go, the magic of the circus (invented here in 1768) goes with them.

We should be fighting to protect this unique part of our cultural heritage—including the animals.

Horse shows and dog trials are allowed on the same commons where circuses are forbidden to pitch.

Circus people are an endangered species and nomads with their own language—Parlari—a mix of English backslang, Italian, Yiddish and Romany.

However, instead of being protected, they are hounded and picked upon by powerful, multi-million-pound organisations, such as Born Free.

More than 200 councils have banned circuses with animals from their parks.

Meanwhile, horse shows and dog trials are allowed on the same commons where circuses are forbidden to pitch.

The Olympics has performing horses, but I don't see a call for dressage to be outlawed.

Circuses are heavily regulated. The report of the Government's Circus Working Group in 2007, in which Born Free was involved, did not see the need for further legislation and did not recommend an end to animals in circuses.

And though it calls for a boycott, the RSPCA inspects every circus with animals when it arrives at a new pitch.

Martin Lacey is more than happy for the inspectors to assess his animals and check their conditions, even though they have no legal right to do so.

'The inspectors on the ground are usually sensible people,' he told me, leaning against a camel. 'They come along, look at the animals and compliment us on the way we care for them.'

Then, he said, they go away blaming the 'official policy' for this dislike of the circus. 'It's head office that's the problem,' they say.

There was a time when circuses weren't persecuted, but celebrated as they came into town. And despite all the politically correct protests, people continue to flood to the Big Top.

There's simply no entertainment like it—the brilliant colours, familiar drum roll and pungent smell of the sawdust.

I wish I could run away to the circus again. I miss riding Julia, feeling her swaying beneath me as if I were in a small boat on a gentle sea.

I miss her tickling me with the tip of her trunk, in search of treats in my pockets. I miss being that close to other animals.

And despite the best efforts of the killjoys, the image of the circus, if not the reality, is still part of growing up.

My children's storybooks have pictures of sealions balancing striped balls on their noses.

My seven-year-old daughter's duvet has pictures of the Big Top with lions and tigers, though she has never watched the real thing. I hope she'll get the chance one day soon. But if Born Free has its way, she never will.

Horse Racing Is Not Cruel

Tim Morris

Tim Morris is director of equine science and welfare at the British Horseracing Authority.

Is it cruel to hit an animal with a whip? If you stopped a passerby in the street and asked them this question their instinctive reply would probably be that it is. It's a natural human response to feel that you shouldn't hit an animal, on the basis that to do so would probably cause unnecessary pain. That is exactly what the British Horseracing Authority (BHA)—the regulator for racing in Great Britain—found when we asked polling organisation SMG/YouGov to put this question to the public.

The Whip

The BHA this week published a landmark review into the use of the whip in our sport. One of the review's key findings is that under a very specific set of circumstances—including the use of an energy-absorbing whip and strict controls on how it can be used—the whip does not cause pain to racehorses and is not cruel. In fact, the whip plays a key role in good horsemanship, and is important to the safety of both the horse and its rider.

Understandably, this is an emotionally charged issue. The public do not like the idea of horses being hit with a whip in the name of sport. The central principle behind the BHA's approach, however, has been that decisions on how we safeguard animal welfare in all aspects of life—including but not limited to sport—should be based on more than just an instinctive response. Rather, a responsible regulator should tackle the complexities of the issue head on and make tough decisions backed with sound empirical evidence.

So with this in mind, the BHA, as part of the review, commissioned in-depth public opinion research (going well beyond the sort of vox pop described above, which is at best simplistic and at worst, biased) in order to better understand people's views on this issue.

The results make very interesting reading. For example, when asked for their instinctive view, 57% of those questioned felt the use of the whip should be completely banned in racing. However, when provided with information about the strict controls that are placed on how (and how often) jockeys can use of the whip, and its role in safely steering and rebalancing an extremely heavy, fast-moving animal, this number came down to 33%. What we believe this indicates is that while some people (in this study 33%), feel that using a whip on a horse can never be justified, for the majority there is a clear acceptance that the whip can and should be used, providing the right controls are in place.

An animal welfare approach is based on the idea that wherever we use animals ... we should make sure strict rules are in place and that animals are well looked after at all times. This is the approach currently taken by racing.

No Pain

The BHA also looked very closely at the animal welfare science behind the effects of the whip on horses in the specific context (and this is important) of adrenaline-fueled race conditions. What we found was that under such conditions, when a horse is in a state of high physiological and mental excitement, the use of an energy-absorbing whip does not cause pain if used within strict limits. In sports science this is often termed 'sportsman's analgesia', and it means that while the whip stimulates a horse during a race, it won't cause pain or suffering if used properly.

Such research has important implications for racing, and one of the recommendations of our review is that training for jockeys takes into account the latest scientific evidence. However, there is also a wider debate taking place here between two different approaches to the role of animals in society.

An animal welfare approach is based on the idea that wherever we use animals—whether in sport, for food, or in groundbreaking medical research—we should make sure strict rules are in place and that animals are well looked after at all times. This is the approach currently taken by racing, and that approach is backed by respected animal welfare organisations such as the RSPCA, SSPCA and World Horse Welfare.

In contrast, an animal rights approach is based on the view that animals should not be used in any way by humans. Those who take this approach feel that sports like racing should be banned and the use of animals in all medical experiments prohibited—even if millions of human lives could be saved through such research.

The BHA's review is a positive step forward for those who support a welfare approach to the role of animals in our lives. As a responsible regulator we have taken the view that the current rules and penalties around the use of the whip are simply not good enough and can be both improved and made clearer.

The changes we have outlined will significantly enhance welfare standards within the sport. We have announced measures that reduce the number of times a jockey can use his or her whip during a race and significantly ramps up the penalties for jockeys who breach the rules. Prize money will be withheld from jockeys who break the rules (if the offence results in a suspension of three days or more) and repeat offenders will face increased penalties and potential loss of their licence to race. The new system will be unambiguous and will provide sufficient disincentive to ensure that jockeys stick to the rules.

There will always be those who feel uncomfortable with the idea of the whip being used in racing. It's up to the sport to be confident in its approach and to explain clearly why, with the right regulation in place, the whip has an important role to play in upholding the highest animal welfare standards.

Outrage over Cockfighting Is Hypocritical and Overblown

Harry Cheadle

Harry Cheadle is a senior staff writer at Vice *magazine.*

This week [March 2013], a Utah state senator named Allen Christensen made news by voting against a bill that would turn cockfighting from a misdemeanor into a felony. (It's already a felony in most of the US.) The reasons he gave included: A) The birds "naturally want to do this thing in their lives," and B) Utah allows women to have abortions, so why doesn't it allow people to strap knives to roosters' claws and get them to cut each other to pieces for entertainment? Obviously, Christensen is being a troll here, and he's probably the kind of guy who mentions abortion when you ask him to pass the potatoes ("UNBORN FETUSES MURDERED BY THEIR LIBRUL MOTHERS CAN'T PASS ANYTHING TO ANYONE BECAUSE THEY'RE DEAD!"), but the story got me thinking: What if there's a sliver of a point here? Why *do* we want to send people who run cockfighting rings to prison?

Chickens Suffering

Let's first go to the Humane Society, who have a pretty good definition of what cockfighting is and why you should want it banned . . . :

> In a cockfight, two roosters fight each other to the death while people place bets. Cockfighters let the birds suffer untreated injuries or throw the birds away like trash afterwards. Besides being cruel, cockfighting often goes hand in hand with gambling, drug dealing, illegal gun sales and murder.

Left to themselves, roosters almost never hurt each other badly. In cockfights, on the other hand, the birds often wear razor-sharp blades on their legs and get injuries like punctured lungs, broken bones and pierced eyes—when they even survive.

Sadly, people often bring young children to cockfights. Seeing adults relish such brutality can teach kids to enjoy violence and think that animal suffering is okay.

Cockfighting happens in many kinds of neighborhoods and in states around the country. It is illegal in all states and a felony in 39, which means that many states need to toughen up their laws.

Obviously, yes, cockfighting is a barbaric blood sport, and if roosters are capable of conscious thought, they are almost definitely not like, *Hell yeah, I want to get cut up by some other rooster with knives on his claws, while drunk humans shout at me!* But if American lawmakers want to start passing bills that reflect a concern for poultry, maybe they should start with the 9 billion chickens that are killed and turned into food every year in the US. While a few of those birds no doubt live happy lives roaming around farmyards and pecking at the dirt, many more of those chickens have lives like this: [picture of chickens in crowded conditions not included].

It seems like the existing laws, plus people not being as cool with animals killing each other for our entertainment as they used to be, are wiping cockfighting out.

Now, bringing up chicken farms as an argument in favor of cockfighting is bull ... —it's like saying, "This bad thing may not be so bad because some other bad thing is also happening." Ideally, we would not routinely abuse animals for entertainment *or* because we want cheap meat at the grocery store. But it's pretty clear that people are totally OK with animal cruelty in general, as long as it's a passive, easy-to-ignore kind of cruelty, like jamming chickens into tiny cages and abusing pigs. . . . Cockfighting, like cat juggling, isn't just cruel, it's so barbaric that it *feels* like we should get rid of it. Those less visible forms of animal mistreatment affect many more animals than cockfighting—as far as I can tell from online research, there are just thousands of birds in the US cockfighting circuit. It's a fairly nasty hobby to have, but it's not exactly a national epidemic.

Bad People?

Besides animal cruelty, the other common complaint against cockfighting is that the people who do it are "bad people." As the Humane Society says, "Cockfighting often goes hand in hand with gambling, drug dealing, illegal gun sales, and murder." That might be true, but should we start banning activities because they're associated with crimes? Should we ban hanging out at bus stations at night? Because I'm pretty sure all of the crimes the Humane Society links to cockfighting go on at Greyhound stations all the time. (And do we really care *that* much about people betting on the fights?)

Changing cockfighting from a misdemeanor to a felony, as Utah is doing, is a convenient way for lawmakers to say that they don't like the sport, but it seems like the existing laws, plus people not being as cool with animals killing each other for our entertainment as they used to be, are wiping cockfighting out. (The *New York Times* reported on cockfighting's decline back in 2008.) Even if cockfighting got legalized, as this Abraham Lincoln-quoting online petition advocates, I doubt we'd start seeing roosters strutting and clawing each other on ESPN2. The sport is going to die out in the US eventually, even without showy police raids. . . .

What happens to the cocks after they get "rescued" in operations like that, by the way? Oh, right: "Almost all roosters seized from cockfighting operations have to be put down because they can't be around other roosters or birds without attacking them." Man, it sure sucks to be poultry in the US, huh?

Organizations to Contact

The editors have compiled the following list of organizations concerned with the issues debated in this book. The descriptions are derived from materials provided by the organizations. All have publications or information available for interested readers. The list was compiled on the date of publication of the present volume; the information provided here may change. Be aware that many organizations take several weeks or longer to respond to inquiries, so allow as much time as possible.

American Anti-Vivisection Society (AAVS)
801 Old York Rd., Suite 204, Jenkintown, PA   19046-1611
(215) 887-0816
e-mail: aavs@aavs.org
website: www.aavs.org

The American Anti-Vivisection Society (AAVS) is a nonprofit animal advocacy and educational organization dedicated to ending experimentation on animals in research, testing, and education. Its website includes extensive information about current practices as well as alternatives to the use of animals in research and education.

American College of Laboratory Animal Medicine (ACLAM)
96 Chester St., Chester, NH   03036
(603) 887-2467 • fax: (603) 887-0096
website: www.aclam.org

The American College of Laboratory Animal Medicine (ACLAM) advances the humane care and responsible use of laboratory animals through certification of veterinary specialists, professional development, education, and research. Its website includes information about career pathways and mentoring, as well as position statements on topics such as adequate veterinary care, animal experimentation, rodent surgery, and pain and distress.

Association of Zoos and Aquariums (AZA)

8403 Colesville Rd., Suite 710, Silver Spring, MD   20910-3314
(301) 562-0777 • fax: (301) 562-0888
website: www.aza.org

The Association of Zoos and Aquariums (AZA) is a nonprofit organization dedicated to the advancement of zoos and public aquariums and to conservation, education, science, and recreation. AZA publishes *CONNECT* magazine, and issues are available on its website. Its website also includes educational resources, information about animal care and management, and other information.

Center for Agricultural and Rural Development (CARD)

Iowa State University, 578 Heady Hall, Ames, IA   50011-1070
(515) 294-1183 • fax: (515) 294-6336
website: www.card.iastate.edu

The Center for Agricultural and Rural Development (CARD) is an academic organization connected to Iowa State University. It conducts public policy and economic research on agricultural, environmental, and food issues. Its website includes numerous articles on animal disease and public opinion of the agricultural industry.

Greenpeace USA

702 H Street NW, Washington, DC   20001
(800) 326-0959 • fax: (202) 462-4507
e-mail: info@wdc.greenpeace.org
website: www.greenpeaceusa.org

Greenpeace USA opposes nuclear energy and the use of toxic chemicals and supports ocean and wildlife preservation. It uses controversial direct-action techniques and strives for media coverage of its actions in an effort to educate the public. It publishes the quarterly magazine *Greenpeace* and numerous books, fact sheets, and reports, many of which are available on its website.

The Humane Society of the United States

2100 L St. NW, Washington, DC   20037
(202) 452-1100
website: www.humanesociety.org

The Humane Society of the United States rescues and cares for animals and conducts advocacy and education to reduce animal suffering and create meaningful social change for animals. It monitors enforcement of existing laws and educates the public about animal issues. The organization's website includes resources for the animal care community, parents, educators, and students. Publications on the organization's website include the magazines *All Animals*, *Kind News*, and *Animal Sheltering*.

National Institutes of Health (NIH)

9000 Rockville Pike, Bethesda, MD   20892-7982
(301) 496-1776 • fax: (301) 402-0601
e-mail: NIHinfo@od.nih.gov
website: www.nih.gov

The National Institutes of Health (NIH) is a branch of the US Department of Health and Human Services and the country's medical research agency; it is also the largest source for medical funding in the world. It sets policy, makes grants, and monitors ongoing research involving both humans and animals. The NIH website contains a section devoted to animals in research, including resources for the general public. Topics covered include basics of medical research with animals, alternatives to research with animals, animal welfare, and information for students and educators.

National Shooting Sports Foundation (NSSF)

11 Mile Hill Rd., Newtown, CT   06470
(203) 426-1320
website: www.nssf.org

The National Shooting Sports Foundation (NSSF) is the trade association for the firearms industry. Its mission is to promote, protect, and preserve hunting and the shooting sports through research, advocacy, and other means. Its website includes news, blogs, research reports, and industry guides related to all forms of hunting.

People for the Ethical Treatment of Animals (PETA)
501 Front St., Norfolk, VA 23510
(757) 622-7382 • fax: (757) 622-0457
website: www.peta.org

People for the Ethical Treatment of Animals (PETA) is an international animal rights organization that works to establish and protect the rights of all animals. PETA promotes public education, cruelty investigations, animal rescue, and legislative action. It produces fact sheets, brochures, flyers, and a weekly e-newsletter. Many of these publications are available on its website.

US Department of Agriculture (USDA)
1400 Independence Ave. SW, Washington, DC 20250
(202) 720-2791
website: www.usda.gov/wps/portal/usda/usdahome

The US Department of Agriculture (USDA) is the US government agency responsible for developing and executing US farm policy. Its website includes news updates, reports, and publications such as *Agriculture Fact Book*. The website includes many articles about humane treatment of animals in agriculture.

Bibliography

Books

Tom L.
Beauchamp and
R.G. Frey, eds.
The Oxford Handbook of Animal Ethics. New York: Oxford University Press, 2014.

Gary L. Francione
and Robert
Garner
The Animal Rights Debate: Abolition or Regulation? New York: Columbia University Press, 2010.

Robert Gamer
A Theory of Justice for Animals: Animal Rights in a Nonideal World. New York: Oxford University Press, 2013.

Jeremy R. Garrett
The Ethics of Animal Research: Exploring the Controversy. Boston: MIT Press, 2012.

Temple Grandin
and Catherine
Johnson
Animals Make Us Human: Creating the Best Life for Animals. Boston: Houghton Mifflin Harcourt, 2010.

Lori Gruen
Ethics and Animals. New York: Cambridge University Press, 2011.

Hal Herzog
Some We Love, Some We Hate, Some We Eat: Why It's So Hard to Think Straight About Animals. New York: HarperCollins, 2010.

Richard Hummel
Hunting and Fishing for Sport: Commerce, Controversy, Popular Culture. Madison, WI: Popular Press, 1994.

Nathan Kowalsky, ed.	*Hunting, Philosophy for Everyone: In Search of the Wild Life.* Malden, MA: Blackwell Publishing, 2010.
Christopher Leonard	*The Meat Racket: The Secret Takeover of America's Food Business.* New York: Simon & Schuster, 2014.
Charles J. List	*Hunting, Fishing, and Environmental Virtue: Reconnecting Sportsmanship and Conservation.* Corvallis: Oregon State University Press, 2013.
Vaughan Monamy	*Animal Experimentation.* New York: Cambridge University Press, 2012.
David E. Newton	*The Animal Experimentation Debate: A Reference Handbook.* Santa Barbara, CA: ABC-CLIO, 2013.
Maureen Ogle	*In Meat We Trust: An Unexpected History of Carnivore America.* Boston: Houghton Mifflin Harcourt, 2013.
Paul Waldau	*Animal Rights: What Everyone Needs to Know.* New York: Oxford University Press, 2011.

Periodicals and Internet Sources

Gene Baur	"Factory Farming Is Not the Best We Have to Offer," *National Geographic,* October 13, 2011. www.newswatch.nationalgeographic.com.
Jeremy Bernfeld	"'In Meat We Trust' Argues We Got the Meat Industry We Asked For," National Public Radio, December 9, 2013. www.npr.org.

Scott Bestul   "Time Magazine Cover Story Should Challenge Deer Hunters," *Field and Stream*, January 2, 2014.

Cody Carlson   "The Ag Gag Laws: Hiding Factory Farm Abuses from Public Scrutiny," *Atlantic*, March 20, 2012.

John Ericson   "The Price of Killing Off Animal Testing," *Newsweek*, February 20, 2014. www.newsweek.com.

Jason G. Goldman   "Ethics at the Zoo: The Case of Marius the Giraffe," *Scientific American*, February 13, 2014. www.blogs.scientificamerican.com.

Chris Hogg   "Understanding Japan's Whale Ethics," BBC News, January 22, 2008. www.bbc.co.uk.

Jennifer Horton   "Are Zoos Good or Bad for Animals?," HowStuffWorks, n.d. (accessed July 18, 2014). www.animals.howstuffworks.com.

Shaoje Huang   "Interest Grows in Animal Testing Alternatives," *New York Times*, May 2, 2014. http://sinosphere.blogs.nytimes.com.

Will James   "Killing Wildlife: The Pros and Cons of Culling Animals," *National Geographic*, March 5, 2014. www.news.nationalgeographic.com.

Louisa Lombard   "Blame War, Not Safaris," *New York Times*, June 29, 2014.

Robin McKie "Ban on Primate Experiments Would Be Devastating, Scientists Warn," *Guardian*, November 1, 2008.

Tiziana Moriconi "Italian Scientists Fight Back on Animal Testing," *Nature*, June 3, 2013.

Nature "Animal Rights and Wrongs," February 23, 2011.

Richard Pollock "Animal Rights Groups That Paid Circus $15.7 Million File Suit Against Insurers Who Cancelled Them in 2000," *Washington Examiner*, July 7, 2014.

Hannah Sentenac "Is the Ringling Brothers Circus Abusing Its Animals in Miami?," *Miami New Times*, January 11, 2013. www.blogs.miaminewtimes.com.

Wesley J. Smith "Why Humanists Should Oppose Animal Rights," *National Review*, January 17, 2014. www .nationalreview.com.

Oliver Wainwright "London Zoo's New Tiger Territory? Built for the Animals First, and Visitors Second," *Guardian*, March 20, 2013.

Bryan Walsh "As Harvard Closes a Primate Research Center, Are Lab Chimps Becoming a Thing of the Past?," *Time*, April 24, 2013.

Gene Weingarten "Down on the Factory Farm," *Washington Post*, September 20, 2013.

Index

H

I

J

K

9 780737 772081